THE BEDFORD WAY SERIES

QUALITY ASSURANCE AND ACCOUNTABILITY IN HIGHER EDUCATION

EDITED BY

CARI LODER

Contributors:
Richard Lewis, Cari Loder, Pauline Perry, Philip Reynolds,
Gareth Williams, Peter Wright

KOGAN PAGE

Published in association with
The Institute of Education, University of London

First published in 1990 by Kogan Page Ltd.,
120 Pentonville Road, London N1 9JN

Typeset by Saxon Printing Ltd., Derby.
Printed and bound in Great Britain by Biddles Ltd, Guildford

British Library Cataloguing in Publication Data

A CIP record for this book is available from the British Library.

ISBN 1-85091-888-0

Contents

Notes on Contributors

Richard Lewis is presently Deputy Chief Executive at the Council of National Academic Awards. He was formerly Head of Department of Accountancy and Taxation at the City of London Polytechnic, Julian Hodge Professor of Accountancy at the University College of Wales, Aberystwyth and Assistant Director, Middlesex Polytechnic. He has also been a visiting professor at the University of Washington, Seattle. At the CNAA he has taken particular responsibility for the establishment of its Credit Accumulation Transfer scheme, its work on the Recognition of Access Courses and the development of its information dissemination activities.

Cari Loder is a researcher in the Centre for Higher Education Studies, Institute of Education, University of London. Her recent research has included an evaluation of new funding mechanisms in higher education, the scope and role of business funding of higher education, and a review of the research and literature on teaching quality in higher education. She has acted as consultant to the European Cultural Foundation, the PCFC and CHEPS and has participated in consultancies for the World Bank, OECD, ESRC and DES.

Pauline Perry is the Director of South Bank Polytechnic, and was formerly Chief Inspector for General Higher Education and Teacher Training in Her Majesty's Inspectorate. Before joining the Inspectorate, she was a university lecturer in Philosophy.

Philip Reynolds was Vice-Chancellor of Lancaster University from 1980 to 1985 and chairman of the CVCP Academic Standards Working Party between 1983 and 1986. Formerly he was Professor of Politics at Lancaster University and Wilson Professor of International Politics at University College of Wales. His publications include *British Foreign Policy in the Inter-War Years* (1954); *An Introductuion to International Relations* (1972); and *The Historian as Diplomat: Charles Kingsley Webster and the United Nations* (1976, with E J Hughes).

Gareth Williams is Professor of Educational Administration and head of the Centre for Higher Education Studies at the Institute of Education, University of London. Before that he was Professor of Educational Planning at Lancaster University. He has worked at the

Organization for Economic Co-operation and Development (OECD), Oxford University and the London School of Economics, as well as doing consultancy work for UNESCO, ILO, the World Bank, and the DES. His books and articles cover many aspects of the economics of education and educational planning with particular emphasis on higher education.

Peter Wright is Higher Education Advisor at the Training Agency, on secondment from Portsmouth Polytechnic. He has published numerous articles including: 'Access or Inclusion: Some comments on the history and future prospects of continuing education in England', *Studies in Higher Education*, 14 (1), 23–40; 'Putting Learning at the Centre of Higher Education' in O Fulton (Ed.), *Access and Institutional Change* (SRHE/OU Press, 1989). He is joint editor of *Higher Education Quarterly*. His research interest lies in the professionalization of knowledge in higher education.

Preface
Cari Loder

Apart from finance, questions of 'quality' and 'accountability' in higher education are inevitably going to be the principal themes in the higher education policy debate in future years. Issues such as accountability to students, meeting the needs of industry and other employers, maintaining academic standards and financial accountability to the government and funding bodies will attract much attention as competition between institutions for students becomes much more severe in the early 1990s.

There has already been much debate on issues such as who should higher education be accountable to and what is meant by 'quality'. Concern is now shifting towards much more practical issues such as who should be the judges of quality? How should quality be rewarded? How can poor quality teaching or research be improved? Can we develop qualitative performance indicators of higher education output?

One view is that the policy interest by government in issues of quality and academic standards mirrors the recently revived concern for quality in British manufacturing industry. Certainly issues of marketing and quality are linked. There are also concerns about student dissatisfaction with courses in terms of both content and presentation; certainly also pressures for rationalization and restructuring call for criteria on which to base administrative or financial interventions.

This monograph examines questions of quality assurance and public accountability in British higher education. The issues examined include the case for a higher education inspectorate. Pauline Perry considers that the ultimate determinant of quality in any institution lies within the institution itself. She states that the quality of institutional management, and the ability of those who manage, to give widespread ownership of goals, and an ethos of quality control, throughout all the activities of the institution is of paramount importance. She believes that if such internal quality assurance mechanisms are in place then it can only be advantageous to also have external and independent evaluators of quality such as Her Majesty's Inspectorate, the Council for National Academic Awards and the universities' Academic Audit Unit.

Philip Reynolds considers whether an external examiner system is an adequate guarantee of academic standards and suggests the following conclusions. First, the external examiner system has little to offer in relation to the academic standards of the higher education system or of individual institutions within it. He maintains that, as far as institutions are concerned, their quality and standards should be judged in relation to the educational purposes of the whole institution: this may have social, physical, broadly cultural, aesthetic, or spiritual as well as intellectual components; and external examiners relate only to the last of these.

However, he concludes that within the context of other procedures that have recently been developed and with the enhanced and more clearly defined role of the external examiners themselves the system, if well operated in an encouraging and stimulating as well as critical way, can make the biggest single contribution to the maintenance and improvement of academic standards.

In his chapter Richard Lewis examines the changing role of the Council for National Academic Awards and whether their role should be extended. He makes the point that the frontiers of higher education are not fixed and that higher education takes place not only in polytechnics, colleges and universities but also in industry and commerce, charitable and religious establishments and in government. One of the great strengths of the CNAA is that its flexibility allows it to respond to requests from a very wide range of organizations who wish to be able to offer CNAA awards.

He draws our attention to the important point that innovation must be balanced with quality. Too rigid an adherence to outmoded views of quality is likely to inhibit change, but too rapid an introduction of change without concerns of quality will produce a sub-standard product.

In her discussion of the role of a national staff appraisal programme as a means of assuring quality, Cari Loder suggests that it serves three main purposes; to maintain and improve teaching and learning; to reinforce a sense of responsibility and allay possible public misgiving and to raise the quality of performance to cope with change and aid in decision making

Although few academics would object to the above aims there is a great deal of unease about the introduction of a university-wide appraisal programme. Uncertainty about the purpose of staff appraisal, lack of motivation on the part of staff to participate in appraisal, institutional difficulties with implementing effective appraisal systems (selecting appropriate appraisers, providing resources for training appraisers and providing effective staff development etc.) all serve to undermine enthusiasm for what should have been a well-received innovation.

She suggests that for appraisal to be an effective means of improving quality it must be linked to a system of institutional and, more importantly, personal rewards. At present there is little or no incentive for academic staff to take seriously the issue of improving their teaching.

One of the very few examples of curricular development in British higher education is the Enterprise in Higher Education initiative. Peter Wright lucidly explains how, by its emphasis on explicit outcomes, accountability, and the involvement of new partners, EHE has thrown revealing light on the central issues that British higher education will have to address if it is to reinterpret its mission to meet the challenges of its rapidly changing environment. He states that EHE has already begun to stimulate new definitions of quality and of the criteria for evaluating them.

Gareth Williams places the issues of quality and accountability firmly in a system-wide context. He proposes that a viable system of quality assurance for the 1990s would be one in which institutions are themselves responsible for ensuring minimum quality thresholds. They would have a collective interest in monitoring the arrangements of individual institutions to ensure that long-term prospects for the sector as a whole were not being undermined by quality short-cuts in individual institutions. However, he believes that responsibility for stimulating and rewarding specific examples of high quality teaching would need to be with the funding councils.

It is possible to envisage funding of innovation and quality improvement and subsidy of worthwhile courses for which student demand is insufficient, as the main resource allocation functions of the funding councils before the end of the century. Indeed it is possible to go further and envisage the main function of universities and polytechnics as institutions as being the assurance of quality in courses and other activities in departments that are effectively financially autonomous operating units.

Chapter One
The Importance of Quality and Quality Assurance
Gareth Williams and Cari Loder

An international comparison

In any critical review of quality in British higher education it is important to recognize that this is one area of economic activity where Britain is still internationally recognized as providing high quality and good value for money. A recent special issue of the widely read but serious French magazine *Liberation* reported the results of a Europe-wide survey to identify the continent's leading higher education institutions in 21 subject areas. The survey was concerned with general academic standing and thus with teaching at least as much as research. Several of the institutions mentioned are not research establishments.

Table 1.1 shows the aggregated results for the three countries most frequently mentioned. It is clearly dangerous to give too much weight to this kind of beauty contest but the high proportion of British institutions mentioned in nearly all subject areas is a matter for some satisfaction and should not be forgotten when considering the self-criticism and proposals for reform in the rest of this book. The aim is to help protect a successful system and to help make it even better, not to offer apologetics for failure. It is in the national interest that, in currently popular terminology, our higher education courses should continue to have an up-market image. It is not just a matter of overseas student recruitment, though at 6 per cent of university income this is not something that can be ignored. Higher education needs to maintain its quality primarily because it is one of the keys to national success as well as individual fulfilment in the information rich society of the twenty-first century.

Quality and accountability

Issues of quality and accountability in higher education are closely related. Accountability involves rendering some form of account that an activity is being carried out effectively and efficiently. Those who are affected by it are entitled to demand that it be carried out effectively and those who provide the resources have a right to see that they are used efficiently. But higher education is not an easy activity to evaluate. Outputs and processes are many and complex. There is no simple relationship between inputs and outputs and it is subject to many random influences. Little is really known about the association between teaching and learning or between scientific research and scientific discovery, or between discovery and application.

Apart from the perennial concern with finance, questions of 'quality' and 'accountability' will be the principal themes in the higher education policy debate in the 1990s. Issues such as accountability to students, meeting the needs of industry and other employers, maintaining academic standards and financial accountability to the government and funding bodies will attract increasing attention as competition between institutions for students becomes more severe.

Table 1.1 Leading universities of Europe

Subject	(1)	Percentage of Mentions			Number in First 3		
		UK	France	Germany	UK	France	Germany
Medicine	5	60%	20%	20%	3	0	0
Economics	10	50%	30%	10%	2	1	0
Archaeology	10	50%	10%	20%	2	1	0
Geology	6	50%	13%	17%	2	1	0
Management	5	40%	20%	0%	1	1	0
Physics	10	40%	30%	20%	1	2	0
Agriculture	13	38%	15%	23%	1	1	0
Sociology	8	38%	38%	13%	1	1	1
Geography	11	36%	9%	9%	2	1	0
Mathematics	15	33%	20%	7%	2	1	0
Biology	15	33%	20%	13%	2	0	1
Tourism Studies	9	33%	22%	11%	2	0	0
Law	20	30%	20%	20%	2	1	0
Political Science	17	29%	12%	18%	2	1	0
Finance	14	29%	29%	14%	0	2	0
History	15	27%	13%	33%	1	1	0
Chemistry	15	27%	20%	27%	2	1	0
Psychology	20	20%	10%	10%	1	1	0
Engineering	22	18%	27%	23%	1	1	0
Architecture	12	17%	0%	33%	1	0	0
Fine Arts	6	17%	17%	17%	1	1	0

Note (1) Number of Institutions mentioned
Source Estimated from information in
      Les 100 Meilleures Universités en Europe
      (Les Guides Liberation No.1: Liberation, Paris), December 1989

The debate about the nature of accountability and the form it should take is, therefore, wide-ranging. It is well established that many academics, particularly those from universities, believe that their prime loyalty is to their academic discipline and that accountability to peers within the discipline ought to be the chief consideration. However, higher education institutions are in some sense accountable to students and their families, to employers and to taxpayers who pay a substantial, though declining, proportion of the bills. There is social and political accountability which is concerned with issues such as ensuring that higher education is accessible to those who are likely to be able to benefit from it. There is financial accountability which is about the efficient use of resources and there is quality accountability which is concerned with promise and performance and the relationship between them.

Challenges to quality

Change and financial stringency inevitably give rise to concern about purposes, quality, performance appraisal, and value for money. In higher education quality is not easily assessed, especially by students and other consumers, and it is almost impossible for them to make reliable judgements before they have experienced it. Quality assurance mechanisms are essential and have always existed in British higher education institutions in three main ways. One is through the professional integrity of individuals and small groups. Under this model blatant breaches of professional codes are usually dealt with very severely but minor peccadilloes are often ignored. Such individual self-regulation is put under considerable strain if competition for resources rewards those who are willing to compromise over quality matters. The second is through the establishment of collective quality assurance procedures. The economic rationale for these is that even though individual academics and even institutions may be able to derive some benefit, at least in the short term, from cutting corners on quality the system as a whole will suffer if in the long run it is perceived as not offering value for money. The third form of quality control is through external incentives and penalties. The experiences of the 1980s clearly demonstrated that higher education responds readily to financial incentives (*vide* Williams 1991) but external quality control of this type is almost invariably bureaucratic and inflexible.

Quality and marketing

In some respects the current interest in issues of quality parallels its revived emphasis in British manufacturing industry during the 1980s.

Marketing and quality are linked. It is being realized that student, or customer, satisfaction with both the form and the substance, the content and the presentation of courses is important. Rationalization and restructuring need criteria on which to base managerial and financial interventions. There is still a widely held view, despite the current buoyant demand for higher education, that the decline in the number of school leavers in the 1990s, will intensify competition for traditional entrants and encourage strategies to increase participation which may in some circumstances put short-term promotional strategy above the maintenance of long-term quality. Whatever forms of public funding finally emerge from the new funding bodies there is inevitably going to be increased competition amongst institutions for students and increased diversity in types of students and courses offered.

An analogy can be made with the Broadcasting Standards Authority and the proposals for a government controlled agency to curb press excesses. Even a government which has a single-minded belief in market competition as the most efficient way of allocating resources recognizes that unrestrained media competition may result in an unacceptable lowering or diversification of standards. It is not inconceivable that higher education, like broadcasting, could have a statutory agency imposed on it if competition for students results in unacceptable practices.

In addition to the possibility of government and funding agencies assuming the task of quality assurance if the system itself is unable to deliver perceived value for money, there is now a real possibility of cost-effective substitutes for existing higher education provision. These might be new privately funded universities or they might be technology based home learning packages.

Likely developments in the 1990s will present two major challenges to quality assurance mechanisms in British higher education. The first is that increasing competition for students may result in a widening gap between what students expect and what they receive. The second is that there will be much greater differentiation of institutions and courses. Already the academic 'gold standard' of the honours degree is no longer synonymous with higher education and its dominant position will almost certainly be eroded during the next decade. A single criterion of excellence, or adequacy, is no longer appropriate. Institutions and courses will need to be judged in terms of their own objectives, rather than standardized external criteria but if quality assurance is to mean anything these objectives will need to be explicitly stated and their implementation monitored.

This book is based on the belief that in a market oriented system of higher education, particularly one in which the government continues to be the main purchaser of academic services, quality assurance mechanisms must be explicit rather than implicit. That while individual professional integrity must remain the cornerstone it should be supported by suitable institution-wide and system-wide procedures and that individuals and institutions should be able to demonstrate their commitment to maintaining and raising the quality of their work in a manner consistent with their recognized objectives.

The binary divide
As always in any discussion of British higher education issues it is important to remember that universities and non-university institutions have very different backgrounds and experiences of quality assurance. For universities the classified honours degree, the invisible colleges of research scientists and institutional self-regulation have been the dominant influences on quality assessment.

There are two distinct characteristics of PCFC institutions which have a direct bearing on the quality of teaching. First, they normally have a close connection with employers and, therefore have, a strong interest in ensuring their courses are up-to-date and adequately meet the needs of industry, commerce and the professions. Second, the function of HMI in relation to polytechnics and colleges helps to remind one that these 'teaching-first' institutions have a tangible commitment to the creation of an ethos conducive to effective teaching and learning by students from a very wide range of educational and social backgrounds.

Conceived as institutions with teaching as their primary concern, the polytechnics and colleges have over many years developed their courses within a demanding national system of quality control, a system based on peer group evaluation and directed towards the collective maintenance of academic standards. During this apprenticeship they have internalized many of the quality control procedures of the national system and in the process have become strong self-evaluating institutions.

Teaching quality and the responsibilities of institutional management
For teaching to be of high quality it is necessary for it to be both *effective* (ie the aims and objectives of the course are met) and *efficient* (the resources used to achieve effectiveness are not excessive). In order to meet these criteria, managers and senior members of any higher education institution need to:

- be clear about its strategic aims and the operational objective against which performance is to be judged in relation to the quality of teaching and learning;
- be familiar with the procedures and processes by which quality and standards are assessed and maintained;
- be able to demonstrate the operational effectiveness of the institution's quality assurance procedures, including the ways in which problems are identified and corrective action taken, and how good practice is identified and disseminated;
- be able to explain the various ways in which the institutional quality assurance procedures relate to external quality control mechanisms;
- be able to show how it analyses the relationships between resource utilization and both the quality of the learning experience of students (process) and the standards they achieve (product);
- be able to demonstrate how the career development needs of staff are identified and how the needs for enhancement of academic and professional qualifications, the improvement of teaching effectiveness and professional and industrial up-dating are met, and how they are prioritized in relation to the aims of the institution and the personal development of staff;
- be able to explain how and in what proportion staff contributions to teaching and to research and scholarship are rewarded and used as a basis for staff development needs;
- be able to demonstrate how the outputs of the various quality control and assurance mechanisms feed back into decision making procedures to ensure appropriate action is taken to maintain and enhance the quality of teaching and learning;
- show how it monitors its quality control and assurance procedures to ensure that they are effective and efficient.

Courses and subjects
For courses as for institutions and the system, the intended purposes of the activity need to be defined before quality can be assessed. Quality has to be judged in the context of fitness for purpose. Aims and objectives need to identify not only the desired outcomes of a course (the skills, abilities and knowledge that the students are expected to achieve), but also the processes and methods to be used – not only what is taught, but how it is taught.

The constituents of good teaching and learning are substantially specific to the structure of the discipline or subject areas and are best identified and evaluated by those close to the discipline. There is a growing literature on the functional, epistemological and cultural differences between various academic subjects and these differences, most recently analysed by Becher (1989) and Squires (1990), clearly have a significant impact not only on the content and sequencing of what is taught but also on teaching methods and the assessment of student learning. On a vocational course in business studies, for instance, teachers are primarily concerned with applied learning; with knowledge, not as an end in itself but knowledge for use. If the main interest is in what students can do with what they know, good teaching will probably be defined in relation to methods which encourage problem-based learning, case studies, project work and placements. On the other hand teaching and learning may be considered as guided, in-depth study of the concepts, structure, processes and criteria of truth which distinguish one discipline from another. Here learning is learning to think like a physicist or an historian, who have quite different disciplinary subcultures; the physicist seeking to establish general propositions and to find recurrent patterns and explain their interconnection in terms of demonstrable laws; the historian interested in particularities and, probably, convinced that in history there are no recurrent patterns and, therefore, no laws. Thus for the historian the detail is at least as important as the universal in any consideration of quality in teaching and learning.

Professionalism and professional control of quality
Teaching can be viewed as labour, craft, profession or art. As profession or art, that is where the appropriate teaching action in relation to the student is complex and cannot be decided by the application of fixed rules, the individual teacher has to use expert judgment in choosing any course of action.

However, while the major responsibility for ensuring the quality of teaching and learning must rest with competent professional and with self-evaluating institutions, it is hard to disagree with the CNAA insistence in its accreditation regulations that the processes and procedures of self-criticism should be open to peer review; that the external examiner system should be strengthened. More controversial is the debate on whether institutions funded by the PCFC should continue to be visited by Her Majesty's Inspectorate and whether, perhaps in some modified form which puts more emphasis on inspection of an institution's own methods of quality control, HMI responsibilities should be extended to the universities.

Accreditation by professional bodies is in some respects an infringement of academic autonomy. It can be justified on the grounds that professional practice necessitates the mastery of certain areas of knowledge and skills whereas a non-professional qualification is simply the result of a 'contract' between the institution and the individual student. However in practice a degree and often class of degree are treated as quasi-professional qualifications. Many employers require the possession of a degree of a certain class as a prerequisite for short-listed candidates and it is virtually impossible for anyone without a minimum of an upper second class honours degree to obtain a Research Council Award. So should not all degrees be subject to the same amount of external regulation as professional qualifications? If not are some applicants being unfairly penalized?

Although quantifiable indicators of performance can and should be developed for the inputs, processes, and outputs of teaching, it is also the case that:

> Institutions of higher education are institutions founded on processes of human interaction and personal development. The language of arithmetic can only offer a crude insight into the effectiveness of these processes.
> (CNAA 1989)

All these distinctions demonstrate that the concept of quality accountability in higher education is not an easy one and that no simple criteria can be established to ensure adherence to rigorous professional and academic standards. To a substantial extent the professional integrity of individual teachers and scholars must remain at the centre of the picture. However, teachers also have a collective responsibility. All members of a discipline accept responsibility to ensure that disciplinary standards are met when they referee for a learned journal and all members of a university or polytechnic should be equally concerned to ensure that all students coming to their institution undergo a certain quality of academic experience commensurate with what they have been led to expect; and that employers of graduates can trust that a particular qualification label carries a consistent, though not necessarily homogenized, message.

The traditional solution to these dilemmas is the external examiner system which at the undergraduate level is almost unique to this country and to those higher education systems that have borrowed heavily from Britain. But it is not at all clear that external examiners can cope when there is great and explicit diversity. Consortia of university and polytechnic departments might well consider the establishment of authorized 'panels' of external examiners with high standing in their fields who would be paid explicitly to undertake the external examining function on a part-time basis. They would at any one time be responsible for similar courses in more than one institution in order to be able to ensure comparability of standards and procedures more easily. Their tasks would include not only moderation of assessment results but also regular course development visits to the departments for which they were responsible.

Quality and funding

The relationship between quality and resource allocation is not unambiguous. Is quality weakness something to be penalized or is it a reason for additional resources to try to overcome the weakness? The UFC and its predecessor the UGC have been explicit as far as research is concerned. University departments with high quality research activity receive extra funds. But there is so far no clear idea of how good quality teaching is best encouraged. In part this is because of problems of appraising teaching quality, and in part a confusion about whether high quality teaching should be rewarded or whether increased resources can and should be used to overcome teaching deficiencies.

A related issue is the relationship between agencies concerned with quality control, and planning bodies. At present the Universities Funding Council has undertaken both quality appraisal (in research) and resource allocation functions, whereas in the public sector quality assessment is shared between HMI, the CNAA and the PCFC. It is widely believed that there will be some convergence of the funding responsibilities of the two councils. Whether this is accompanied by merging of quality assurance arrangements has not yet been considered.

Performance indicators

From all the foregoing it is apparent that it is extremely difficult to establish measures of quality on individual courses in individual institutions and it often proves to be necessary to rely on indirect or partial measures and observations of inputs, outputs, processes or reputations.

The following list represents some of the measures of institutional teaching quality which have been suggested in the literature.

Input measures

- Qualifications of student entrants
- Expenditure per student
- Qualifications and experience of academic staff
- Staff numbers
- Resources (equipment, library etc)

Market performance

- Market share in specific programme areas
- Ratio of applicants to entrants
- Qualifications of entrants (as a measure of popularity)
- Opinions of academic peers
- Intake as a percentage of targets

Process measures

- Progress rates (wastage and completion rates)
- Student choice of elective courses within an institution
- Student appraisal of teaching staff
- Variety, effectiveness and suitability of teaching methods
- Variety, effectiveness and suitability of learning opportunities
- Amount and relationship of research and scholarship to teaching and learning
- Effectiveness of validation and review

Output measures

- Percentages of graduates with each class of degree
- Destinations of graduates (student employability)
- Employer satisfaction
- Student satisfaction

Generating a listing of this kind is relatively easy. However, it is much less easy to translate such lists into useful criteria that can be applied by an institution or a funding body. It has been argued that:

> the most important measure of teaching quality must surely be the standard which students themselves have attained at the end of their course of study. This standard is the most direct and important indicator of the quality of teaching since it represents the outcome or 'product' of department, faculty or institution. (Perry 1987)

However there is a wide variation in the distribution of degree classes both between institutions and within subjects and it is far from proven that there is a direct connection between the quality of teaching and the standard students achieve on examinations.

Another approach is to look beyond the final examination and make the assumption that the real evidence of teaching quality lies in the subsequent performance of graduates and in the skill and knowledge which is at their disposal after they have entered the labour force. However, the validity of first destination statistics has been challenged and, although the evidence of employers is obviously important, it is difficult to gather it systematically and to interpret its significance.

Questionnaires to students can provide information on their satisfaction with their courses, but it is far from clear when the information should be collected and how it can it be used for any purposes other than formative feedback to the staff concerned.

Most performance measures in use or being considered focus on inputs or outputs. This is not entirely satisfactory if student learning is essentially a process. Unless the educational process is appropriate, desired learning outcomes are unlikely to follow. Barnett (1989) argues that quantitative performance indicators are largely irrelevant to the improvement of the quality of learning. He claims that,

> essentially higher education is a developmental process of increasing intellectual maturity, whereby, in their chosen academic or professional fields, students reach a stage at which they are able to think independently, form views of their own, are able to defend their views, and are aware of the essentially limited validity of all knowledge claims. Given this view of higher education, it is difficult to see how performance indicators can be of any help.

Recently some authors have begun to stress the need for suitable measures of value-added showing the relationship between input and output measures, but despite some useful conceptualizations there is little to suggest how the concept might be used in practice. Economists have long used a value-added concept in their calculations of rates of return to higher education, based on comparisons of lifetime earnings of graduates and non-graduates but this is a crude measure and even if refined considerably it is difficult to see how it could help identify the current quality of individual courses. The alternative of devising some form of pre- and post-test examinations based on nationally normalized examinations seems an unlikely prospect.

Cave *et al* (1988), review the literature on value-added systems and conclude 'that research in this area is still in its infancy and by no means at a stage where we can say value-added measures can or cannot be made operational at some level.' The assessment of value-added compounds the problems of finding suitable output measures and there is little point in attempting to develop measures of value-added until accepted output measures are available. Value-added seems likely to remain a concept reminding us that different higher education institutions do different things to different students, and that institutions deserve as much credit for recruiting unpromising students and bringing them up to an acceptable level as others do for taking in the ablest students and turning them into national leaders.

References

Barnett, R.A. (1987) The maintenance of quality in the public sector of the UK higher education. *Higher Education* 16/3, pp.279–301.

Becher, T. (1989) *Academic Tribes and Territories: intellectual enquiry and the culture of disciplines*. Milton Keynes: SRHE/Open University Press.

Booth B., and Booth, C. (1989) Planning for Quality: advice respectfully tendered to the PCFC. *Higher Education Quarterly* Vol. 43 No. 4, pp.278–288.

Cave, M., Hanney, S. and Kogan, M. (1988) *Performance Indicators in Higher Education: a critical analysis of developing practice*. London: Jessica Kingsley.

Council for National Academic Awards (1989) Toward an educational audit. *Information Services Discussion Paper 3*. London: CNAA.

Lindop, Sir N. (Chairman) (1985) *Academic validation in public sector higher education: the report of the Committee of Enquiry into the academic validation of degree courses in public sector higher education*. (Cmnd 9501) London: HMSO.

Perry, P. (1987) Accountability and Inspection in Higher Education. *Higher Education Quarterly* Vo!. 41 No. 4, pp.344–353.

Squires, G. (1990) *First Degree: the undergraduate curriculum*. Milton Keynes: SRHE/Open University Press.

Williams, G. L. (1991 – forthcoming) *New Funding Mechanisms in Higher Education*.

Chapter Two
Is There a Need for a Higher Education Inspectorate?
Pauline Perry

It is to be greatly welcomed that, after a decade of concentrating attention on the quality of research in universities, the 1990s have opened with a well-focussed attempt to devise ways of evaluating the quality of teaching in higher education. Both the Polytechnics and Colleges Funding Council (PCFC) and the Universities Funding Council (UFC) have the remit of teaching quality within their terms of reference, and each has affirmed its determination to take the quality of teaching into account in its work. Professor Stuart Sutherland has recently chaired a committee of the CVCP, whose report recommended the setting up of an Academic Audit Unit, controlled by the universities themselves, and providing a regular review or 'audit' of the quality of teaching in the sector. The PCFC set up a working group on teaching quality, due to report during 1990.

Her Majesty's Inspectorate
The public sector, however, already has a higher education inspectorate in Her Majesty's Inspectorate (HMI) from the Department of Education and Science, whose proper role is to inspect the quality of the learning experience provided for students in this sector.

HMI activities have been greatly increased in the polytechnics and colleges during the past few years, resulting in the publication of inspection reports on individual polytechnics, and on the polytechnic sector in England as a whole. In the first round of funding for the 1990/91 financial year, the PCFC relied heavily on HMI advice on quality, in making its funding decisions that were related to quality.

This increased presence of HMI in public sector higher education has had several side effects and benefits. First, it has allowed HMI to be much more public about the methods they use, the criteria by which they judge, and the meanings of the various gradings of quality which they assign during their visits. Just as important, it has provided for the public debate, that element of quality assessment which is unique to HMI: that is the judgement of a body of professionals, who have developed a methodology for the formulation of quality judgements, pooling and balancing these between a team visiting the same department or course in order to provide a 'collective professional judgement'. HMI do not use the research methods of classroom observation. From the first and central professional and informed judgement of quality, they move to analyse and describe the elements which have contributed to the quality – or its absence – in any given classroom, laboratory or workshop episode.

Given the increasing importance of HMI judgements of quality, to the PCFC sector it is useful to examine in some detail exactly how these judgements are reached. At this point it has been most valuable having the public statement by HMI published in the recent PCFC document *Recurrent Funding and Equipment Allocations for 1990/91*. In it HMI do make it clear from the beginning, that their 'prime concern is with standards of learning', and again 'the evaluation of learning is our central purpose'.

Quality and student learning
It is significant that HMI use the word learning, and not the word teaching. This focus is one of the most important insights which HMI have to contribute. Indeed, the document (PCFC 1990) goes on to explain that the quality of teaching is only one of the issues, including organization, management, resources, and quality control arrangements, with which they concern themselves as factors leading in various ways to the quality of the learning outcomes. HMI draw attention to students in higher education to whom we, as providers of higher education, are first and foremost accountable. Our students are our clients, and the quality of learning they achieve is our service to them: but it is also the 'product' which we 'sell' to their future employers. Far too many of the quality control systems which operate in higher education operate outside the level of the classroom, and therefore outside much of the direct experience of students on a day to day basis.

It is, for example, wholly possible for a course to be well-designed, up to date in its thinking and approach, with all the appropriate reading lists as well as course content described in the document, and yet for the quality of teaching on that course to be so poor as to negate the excellent planning. In recognizing this, HMI assess the range and appropriateness of the provision, including the design of the course or courses they are inspecting, but their focus remains on the learning which students are enabled to undertake; on their experience in the classroom; on the assessment which is offered for their work; and on the tasks which are set for them in their private study.

Perhaps the most reassuring, and professionally significant part of HMI's published evidence is the statement that factors other than the quality of teaching itself bear upon the quality of student learning. Most notably, HMI include in this range the overall quality of the staff, including their involvement in research, consultancy and other forms of staff development. Even further, HMI regard the influence of the accommodation, including the furnishings and the equipment, as contributing to 'an appropriately supportive learning environment'. Few of us who manage institutions would disagree with this, although maximum ingenuity is often required to achieve even minimum standards necessary for an appropriate learning environment, in buildings which HMI themselves say, in respect at least of the polytechnics, are seriously deficient in about two-thirds of cases.

The universities' Academic Audit Unit

The universities' Academic Audit Unit (AAU), although in many ways like an Inspectorate, deriving some of its ideas about procedures from the practice of HMI, nevertheless also differs in some important aspects, not least because it also displays some of the good qualities to be found in the new style Council for National Academic Awards (CNAA).

The style of the AAU is therefore much closer to the style of the new CNAA procedures in relation to accredited institutions. As such, it is to be welcomed. There can be few doubts that quality control, and quality assurance, can only be achieved within the institution itself, by the community of people, academic and administrative, who are responsible for the teaching, learning and research. It is therefore absolutely right that the 'external' monitoring should concentrate on ensuring that the institution is performing its own proper job, and that quality control is adequate. As the AAU is also required to obtain evidence from each university of external examiners' reports, student views and the views of external bodies such as the professional accrediting bodies and employers, it seems clear that the AAU procedures will be extremely rigorous. As universities are also to be encouraged to publish the reports which the Unit writes after concluding its audit, the work of quality assurance will also be public, and good practice well disseminated. This should do much to achieve the accountability to the public and the funding council, for which the Unit is designed.

It is however apparent that one major element in which the university sector will continue to differ, is in the emphasis which HMI place in their polytechnic inspections, on the classroom, laboratory or workshop experience of the student. Many, not only in the universities, might argue that this form of inspection is an intrusion on a professional process and as such is neither welcome nor reliable. However, the professional activity of teaching is a public and accountable one, and it is hard to see how lecturers or teachers are in any way different from other professionals whose professional practice is open to public audit and review. Furthermore, I am convinced that the open sharing of the wealth of good practice and excellent teaching which abounds in higher education, would be wholly beneficial of the system, and would in most cases overwhelmingly reassure its critics.

Institutional management systems
The quality of students' learning, however, demonstrably derives not only from the academic activities of teaching, course planning, and fair, valid and reliable examinations. In order to deliver the appropriate level of academic activity, the institutional management, and the administrative systems which exist within the institution, must also work together with academic effort to form the quality 'ethos' which all of us seek. Indeed, the AAU, HMI and the CNAA's excellent process of accreditation for institutions, all now throw an appropriate emphasis on the management systems of quality assurance, which they recognize not only at the point of inspection or accreditation, but which we are now left to maintain, develop and strengthen, in order to exercise the responsibility which we as a community in an academic institution have for our own standards – and which, as I have suggested, no outside agency can ever fully exercise.

It is also good to see that all three systems recognise the importance of evaluating institutional effectiveness against institutional goals. Within an academic management system, I believe the most important responsibility is effective goal setting. Any evaluation of the effectiveness of an institution must first begin by judging it against the goals which we have collectively agreed for ourselves. The senior management of higher education have too often in the past allowed individual academics or small groups to decide for themselves, without any coordination or consensus, what goals we should seek to obtain by the provision of higher education, and I am sure that we have not been wise to do so.

Nor do I believe that the professionals in higher education should set such goals on their own: the academic community should take responsibility for dialogue with employers, students, government, and the wider elements within society, in order to determine how it can best direct its own efforts and expertise towards the needs of those to whom it is ultimately accountable. Within the institution, the existence of adequate structures for setting appropriate goals, and communicating these throughout the institution as a marker against which each individual can judge their own performance, should be an inescapable requirement for us all.

One of the most powerful arguments for taking polytechnics out of the Local Authority sector was the impossibility of any single Local Authority providing an effective interpretation of the many national constituencies to which national institutions must respond. I know of no polytechnic which had not already developed its own effective mechanisms for dialogue with its immediate local community of schools, further education colleges, local industry and the adult community.

I also expect an honest attempt to absorb, describe and evaluate the institutional ethos on the part of any external evaluator. The measure of our success in higher education is the extent to which the ethos of quality control has been determined and made effective inside each institution. The guardians of quality cannot be limited in number or location within the academic community. The delivery of quality must be accepted and owned by all staff, academic, administrative and manual, if it is to be effective, and the evaluation we perform ourselves or which is performed upon us from outside must include some understanding of how far this institutional ethos of quality control has been achieved, in practice as well as on paper.

I can find no objection to the concept of external, objective evaluation of the quality of an institution's outcomes, both academic and financial. We shall no doubt continue to be required, and rightly so, to give full and detailed accounting of ourselves in staff and student statistics, as well as making detailed returns to our funding councils on our stewardship of public property and money. Our ability to do this will of course depend on the effective management systems we have within the institution, and indeed with all such external measures, it is to a large extent the management of the university or polytechnic which is truly being assessed. The setting of appropriate goals; the internal system of quality control; the ethos of the institutions; the good housekeeping in resource terms; the effective marketing of the institution and its products; all these depend on the quality of management, and I would for that reason be very reluctant to embark on any debate which determined these standards for judgement, without defining what is meant by 'good management'.

There is no need to remind academics or administrators that the management of higher education at all levels has been severely criticized in recent years, in reports such as the Jarratt Report (1985) on management in universities, and the National Advisory Body's good management practice report (1984), which heavily criticized the local authorities and their role in public sector higher education. HMI themselves have said in several earlier reports that good management was sadly lacking in the local authority sector of higher education, but have since commented that the management systems developing within the institutions generally provide a sound basis on which to found the new challenges of incorporation.

Government initiatives
The past few years have seen a range of government initiatives, culminating in the 1988 Education Reform Act, which have attempted to tighten up management of universities and polytechnics. For those in the public sector, the Education Act offered a major opportunity for making things better, in that it has taken away the role of the local authority in determining the details of management and administration within institutions. The CNAA's initiative of accreditation and self-validation for institutions is to be welcomed as it has given us the necessary autonomy to manage our academic affairs better.

One of the more dangerous elements of the debate about management in higher education is the commonly held assumption that there is a divide between administrative and academic activity: that one side is concerned with administration and management, whose role is keeping the books straight, keeping the money right, and setting up effective systems of monitoring, recording and assessing all aspects of the institution. The other comprises a set of activities which are academic and which must be left totally free, autonomous and independent, with the assumption that these academic activities are inherently superior to the administrative and management activity.

I feel very strongly that the separation of these two aspects of higher education is going to be fatal if we allow it to be pursued. If we allow management, administration, financial and resource control to be separated from academic purposes and goals, and if we allow the people who pursue those academic goals to see themselves as separate from, and alien to, the new management practices which we are rightly imposing on ourselves, in response to the funding councils and government guidelines, then we run risk of either allowing administrative efficiency to destroy the academic ethos of higher education, or alternatively of allowing academic attitudes and practices to distort and nullify any improvement in management effectiveness.

It is extremely worrying to hear people say with approval that a particular Professor is 'an outstanding academic but of course useless at management'. If academic institutions are to be effective, these two aspects must somehow be welded together. If there is to be effective quality control, in the right sense of the word, then it must be accepted as an integral part of the academic activities of the institution, internalized by the academics themselves.

Quality assurance and quality control depend equally on the right use of resources, the right use of money, the right use of people, the right systems and structures for internal evaluation, if the academic purposes and goals for which higher education institutions exist, are to be realized.

External validation
Many observers have drawn attention to the weakness of some of the external structures of quality control exercised by professional bodies and institutions, and by the external examiner system. Although I would agree that neither the accreditation by a professional body, nor the external examiner system alone are adequate for quality control, I believe they provide important ingredients in a whole network of quality control provided by external inspection of the quality of learning, the internal quality control ethos of the institution, and the use which the institution itself makes of the external examiners' reports, or the professional institutes' comments.

My own experience of the professional institutes is wholly positive. I have found the visitations by the engineering institutes, as well as other professional institutes such as the Committee for Accreditation of Teacher Education, or the Royal College of Nursing, a most positive external input into our own institutional thinking. Their specific role is to say, in general terms, that certain courses fulfil the criteria for producing the types of graduates that the profession desires, and that the graduate from that course is therefore worthy of a licence to practice. They do not and cannot comment on the quality of the student experience or the academic standards which they achieve, as this is not their role. Within their appropriate and limited sphere, I have found them to perform extremely well.

Nevertheless, neither the professional bodies nor the external examiners can provide for the management of the institution that key factor, of an external, neutral judgement of the experience which students have in their day to day learning on a course. I believe we owe it to the constituency of our students, as well as to the constituency of those outside who provide our finances, employ our students, and work with them during their adult lives, to see that the overall quality of the student experience is both appropriate and valuable. This is why there is still an identifiable need for the independent evaluation of the learning experience which an Inspectorate is qualified to undertake, and which neither the AAU in the universities, nor the CNAA in the public sector, sets out to perform.

Her Majesty's Inspectorate, like others inside and outside the institution, are concerned with the range and appropriateness of the provision, and with the quality of the environment and resources. HMI are however crucially concerned with the observation of the quality of learning, that is to say the quality of higher education at the point at which it is delivered to the students. It is the observation of quality at this point performed by outsiders, which is lacking from the other external controls. This does not excuse us internally from better observation and assessment of our own educational provision at the point of delivery to our students, but even the best internal systems which might be set up would still be balanced and complemented by the impartial and experienced observer from outside.

Many have advanced arguments for all evaluation being evaluation of peers, and peer judgement was (mistakenly) believed to be the essence of the old CNAA system pre-1986. Both the universities and the public sector have external evaluation based both on peer judgement and on the judgement of outsiders from many other agencies. The universities' Academic Audit Unit will rely on the part-time involvement of practising academics which will be a strength.

However, HMI's full-time experience of visiting, and evaluating learning in a wide range of institutions, balancing judgements constantly against the judgements of others involved in the same inspection, provides a sound and valuable basis for judgement.

Inspection and evaluation is a very skilled activity in its own right. As the head of an institution I am quite clear that if someone is to tell the government about the health of higher education or to tell the funding body of the health of my institution, I would rather it were HMI or people who worked as HMI do, than a team of people who brought with them, however hard they try to ignore it, their own institutional loyalty and inevitably limited experience. I believe that the universities' Academic Audit Unit may find itself moving in the future in the direction of more full-time evaluators than is currently envisaged.

Conclusion

The ultimate determinant of the quality in any institution, as we are all agreed, is within the institution itself. It is within the quality of the management, and the ability of those who manage, especially at head of department level, to give widespread ownership of goals, and an ethos of quality control, throughout all the activities of the institution. As long as we have such systems of internal quality control and quality assurance in place, I believe it to be wholly to our advantage to have external and independent evaluators of our students' learning experience, to build and strengthen our own institutional performance, and to hold up to us a clear and well polished mirror composed of their unbiased and professional judgement on what we do.

References

Jarratt, A. (Chairman) (1985) *Report of the Steering Committee for Efficiency Studies in Universities*. London: CVCP.

NAB 4 (National Advisory Body for Local Authority Higher Education) (1984) *Quality*. London: NAB (mimeo).

Chapter Three
Is an External Examiner System an Adequate Guarantee of Academic Standards?
Philip Reynolds

The short answer to the question of whether an external examiner system is an adequate guarantee of academic standards is that it is not. But the short answer ignores the fact that the question subsumes two other questions: 'Has an external examiner system been' and 'Might an external examiner system be' an adequate guarantee of academic standards? I shall take these two questions in order.

What is meant by academic standards?

Three preliminary points need to be considered. First, *what do we mean* by academic standards? This requires only brief discussion, because much has been written and said about it since the then Secretary of State for Education and Science, Sir Keith Joseph, raised the issue in a letter to the Chairman of the University Grants Committee in 1983. To my mind standards are best seen as means of measurement of the criteria by which quality may be judged. But quality has no meaning except in relation to purpose. If the purpose of a building is to provide a pleasant environment to live in, then specifications of height, window area, ventilation, heating and so on may be given which will lead to achievement of that purpose. But if the purpose of a building is to stimulate a sense of awe or mystery, as perhaps in a church, then different specifications of height and light will be required and a building of high quality for a church is unlikely to be of high quality for living in.

The question of academic standards is bedevilled by the fact that higher education is seen as having several purposes, and there is no universal agreement on priorities among them. Thus to the committed scholar the quality of higher education is likely to be determined by its ability to produce a steady flow of people with high intelligence and commitment to learning who will continue the process of transmission and advancement of knowledge. To a Secretary of State a high quality system may be one that produces trained scientists, engineers, architects, doctors and so on in numbers judged to be required by society. To an industrialist in the British tradition a high quality educational institution may be one that turns out graduates with wide-ranging, flexible minds, readily able to acquire skills and adapt to new methods and needs. The measurements required, and thus the standards to be applied will be different for each of these notions of quality.

The above paragraph has, however, introduced the second of the preliminary points. The suggestion above is that a Secretary of State may be more likely to be interested in the quality of a whole system, the industrialist in the quality of an individual institution, and the scholar in the quality of a degree programme. These distinctions are not of course wholly exclusive, but they indicate that the notion of quality may be applied at different levels – at the system level, the institutional level and the course or degree programme level – and the notions of quality at each level are likely to be different. The external examiner system operates only at the last of these levels; and while the examiners' quality assessments may relate to scholarship objectives, or to society's needs and objectives, or to employability objectives, or to some mix of these, it would be methodologically hazardous to derive from a chorus of external examiners' assertions of high standards that a whole institution or a whole system was of a high standard. An external examiner system, that is to say, may be able to offer some guarantee of standards at the course or degree programme level, but has little to contribute to assessments of quality at the institutional or system levels.

The third preliminary point is to highlight the adjective 'adequate'. No complete guarantee could ever be given, because many of the criteria of quality cannot be measured exactly but depend on indicators of varying degrees of validity and reliability. Nor indeed would it be wise to attempt as near complete a guarantee as might be imagined: just as a financial control system needs to identify and control all major components of expenditure and income but not to reach down to such as level of detail that the savings made are outweighed by the cost of the operation, so too intensive an attempt at measurement of academic standards could cause the notion of quality to be lost in the process of measurement itself. I return to this below. Let me turn then to the first of the questions subsumed in the title of this chapter.

Has the external system proved an adequate guarantee of standards?
The guarantee sought is that the objectives of the course or degree
programme are adequately achieved. The question is best approached
through a consideration of the duties typically specified for external
examiners, and the context within which those duties were performed.

Thirty years or so ago the duties of external examiners were as often
as not agreed in informal communications among colleagues. The
external examiner normally addressed two questions. First, if internal
marking of the course unit, or the degree programme, suggests an
upper second class honours degree: would this performance result in
an upper second in my institution, or in any other institution in which I
am examining? Second, if student X gets an upper second is it right that
student Y gets a lower second? Those questions quite evidently offer
no adequate guarantee of standards. The questions relate only to
performance on the topics to which the students addressed themselves,
not to the objectives of the course. They provide no measure of
educational experience. They rely on the notion of comparability, but
in fact comparability is highly questionable. There is only limited
comparability between the assessment of a history degree which is
wholly assessed by examination, and a history degree which is assessed
in part by course work and in part by examination. Different things are
being measured. In my own field of International Relations, to seek to
compare an upper second, when the approach was largely philosophi-
cal and historical, with an upper second when the degree programme
relied heavily on statistical methods seems to me a dubious
undertaking.

So of the two traditional duties, one – maintaining equity among
students – could be effectively performed; but the other – ensuring that
classifications in one institution were similar in standard to classifications in others – rested on somewhat shaky foundations in many
subjects, if not perhaps in all. But neither produced an adequate
guarantee of standards, properly defined. There were moreover other
weaknesses, such as the existence of friendships or hostilities among
individuals, particularly heads of department (although I think the
effect of that is often, and easily, exaggerated). Rather more seriously
an external examiner would always find it exceedingly difficult to argue
that a whole classification was wrong. Cases can be identified where an
external examiner was simultaneously acting in two institutions, one of
which was generally highly regarded and the other universally ranked
much lower, and where the examiner found that the assessment level
applied in the supposedly inferior institution was significantly ahead of

the level applied in the more renowned. Even if the examiner judged that the higher level was more appropriate, it would require very strong conviction and authority to bring down the results of most of the students in the latter institution. This may be one of the reasons why a recent enquiry at Hull found historical tradition to be a very strong influence on degree classes in particular institutions. A third comment on the traditional duties would be that the two questions with which externals typically concerned themselves did almost nothing to stimulate review or revision or improvement of courses or of course structures, or of teaching or learning. If suggestions were made there was not normally machinery for seeing whether action had been taken on them.

My answer to the first question would then be that until relatively recently (up to between five and ten years ago) external examiners played an important role in relation to equity among students, an impressionistic but not necessarily wholly ineffective role in relation to comparability among institutions in students' performance in individual subjects, but a small role in relation to maintenance or improvement of standards, and then only of course at the degree not the institution or system levels. Such inadequacies in the monitoring of standards as those noted above were not however equally characteristic of all subjects. By and large the inadequacies were likely to be greatest in those subjects where the subjective element in assessment was high (most of the humanities and the creative arts, some of the social sciences), and least where the assessment was more objectively measurable (engineering, mathematics, most of the sciences).

The context of external examination
As far as the context of operation of the external examiner system is concerned, significant differences existed between most universities on the one hand and institutions in the public sector whose degrees were validated by the CNAA on the other. The typical informality in the universities of appointment of examiners and of specification of their duties has already been noted, but in addition many universities did not have systematic and rigorous procedures for internal monitoring of the educational process although statistical scrutiny of degree results was normal. In the public sector, by contrast, the CNAA laid down detailed requirements for course proposals, scrutinized institutions' internal monitoring procedures, set out formal statements of external examiners' duties and required regular reports from them. Those universities that validated degree programmes in public sector

institutions acted not on dissimilar lines, though their modes of operation were significantly different.

The first requirement for making an external system less inadequate (bearing in mind that the discussion relates only to standards at the course or degree programme level) was thus met in the public sector before it was generally met in universities; that is to say that since quality relates to purpose, the central component of monitoring standards consists in assessing the extent to which the objectives of degree programmes are achieved. Without a formal statement of the intellectual and/or practical skills students were expected to acquire through the degree programme (or the individual course) no judgement of standards could be made. It is now universal practice throughout the university and public sectors of higher education for external examiners to be given a statement of course and degree programme objectives.

A second practice now widely adopted is for the occasion of external examiners' visits to be used for discussion of degree structures and content, and of teaching methods. This assists the dissemination of new ideas and innovative methods and generally promotes good practice. It can lead to significant improvement in achievement of course objectives. Whether discussion of objectives themselves should form part of an external examiners' duties is more debatable; it may be argued that it is for the teachers and the academic authorities in the institution to determine what they wish to do – bearing in mind outside requirements and pressures as well as students' needs – and the task of the external examiner is to judge whether they are doing what they wish to do well, and to help them to do it better, not to judge whether what they are doing is the right thing to do.

Discussion of this kind would in any case take the examiners beyond their role in relation to academic standards and so is outside the scope of this chapter.

The effectiveness of the system
A number of essentially practical or procedural steps can be taken to increase the effectiveness of the external examiner system. The appointment of external examiners should be effectively, and not just formally, scrutinized by a body superior to the department from which proposals will normally come. Examiners' appointments should be for a period sufficiently long for them to gain a good view of the department's work, but not so long that they become effectively in-group members of the department. The appropriate period is probably

between three and five years. Examiners should report annually on their work and their impressions, and these reports should go not, or not only, to the head of department, but to a superior authority within the institution capable of ensuring that appropriate action is taken. To this end the department should report on its action to that authority or to the external examiner or his successor, or if the decision has been to take no action the reason for that decision should be stated.

These routine procedures greatly enhance the effectiveness of the system and are now generally followed. Two other proposals for enhancing effectiveness are more controversial. First, there is widespread but not universal agreement that an external examiner should have the power of veto on any particular course mark or degree classification, now of course in the light of his knowledge of the programme's objectives. Some teachers refuse to accept external examiner duties where their veto power is not explicitly accorded. Some departments maintain *per contra*, that it is not reasonable that one or two persons, with necessarily limited acquaintance with a student's work, should have the power of overriding even the unanimous judgement of teachers who have know the student's work over three or more years. Clearly the examiner's hand is strengthened if the veto power attaches; but whether standards, or equity, are better maintained thereby is likely to vary with personalities and with assessment procedures.

A second controversial, and less commonly adopted, method of enhancing the effectiveness of the system is for the external examiner to select a few students for viva voce examination by him alone, this process being quite separate from vivas used as an aid to classification of candidates on the borderline between classes. Such vivas would not affect the classification of the students concerned (so the students selected should clearly fall within a particular class), but would be intended to give the examiners a feel for the students' educational experience, and to establish a better base for judging the extent to which course objectives were being achieved, and for giving advice about changes that might advantageously be made.

Through arrangements of this kind an external examiner system can effectively influence academic standards. The very existence of such arrangements does of course affect the attitudes and behaviour of teaching members of departments. Nevertheless such as system would not in my view provide by itself an adequate guarantee of standards. It needs to operate as part of a set of other procedures. Among these procedures there should, first, evidently be regular internal and regular review of course objectives, and external examiners might be invited from time to time to participate in such discussions. The value of such reviews can be enhanced by external peer group advice, but clearly this should be sought only at more extended intervals, both for reasons of cost, and in order not to overburden the limited number of experienced members of the profession.

Staff appraisal

A third component of the context of an external examiner system is staff appraisal. It is perhaps understandable that the University Grants Committee found it difficult to develop a national scheme for measurement of teaching performance, but the difficulty in developing a system of teaching appraisal is perhaps less at the institutional level. One indicator of teaching quality (not I think widely used) may be found in the regular analysis of student results in different courses. The existence over a number of years of a pattern of lower student performance in one course as compared with the performance of the same students in others would suggest a deficiency in teaching that needed to be dealt with. To this one can add the sounding of student opinion. An increasing number of departments now make regular use of student questionnaires but many of these I believe are too simple in form. Much better guidance can be obtained from structured questionnaires that require the student to rank objectives and rate performance in relation to them.

Accreditation

One further component of the context of an external examiner system is accreditation, the process by which bodies external to the educational institutions scrutinize degree programmes, and/or prescribe components of these, with a view to certifying that students successfully completing the programme are fit, or with limited further training will be fit, to practice in a profession. There are now 49 such bodies exercising accrediting functions in relation to 34 subject areas. Sometimes the accrediting bodies are restrictive and inhibiting, and make innovation more difficult; the engineering institutions seem particularly to attract this complaint. The General Medical Council by contrast is reported to be more generally constructive and helpful. But whatever the different practices of the accrediting bodies they form an important part of the context within which the external examiner system operates.

National agencies

There remains then one last question that perhaps ought to be addressed. Does an external examiner system of the kind described, operating within a framework of practices such as those just outlined, still provide so inadequate a guarantee of academic standards that it needs to be supplemented by a national agency? Three such agencies now exist – the Academic Audit Unit of the Committee of Vice Chancellors and Principals, the Council for National Academic Awards, and Her Majesty's Inspectorate.

An answer to the question is perhaps to be found in the experience of the new universities founded in the early 1960s and the polytechnics designated in the middle of that decade. For each of the new universities an Academic Advisory Board was established with the duty of vetting proposals for degree programmes and determining that the programmes and their assessment were appropriate for the award of degrees. Within a few years – usually about five – each of the Academic Advisory Boards dissolved themselves, being satisfied that the university had established procedures, and the staff had experience and judgement, sufficient to ensure the maintenance of academic standards.

The polytechnics passed through a longer and more rigorous period of supervision. The Council for National Academic Awards, for whose degrees the polytechnics taught, created a massive system of documentation and visitations to institutions as a means of meeting their prescribed task of ensuring that degrees in the polytechnics (and also in colleges of higher education) were of equivalent standard to those in the universities. There was no other way for a body centred in London to oversee the academic affairs of some hundreds of institutions. It is indisputable that the universities were able to learn a great deal from the practices and procedures that the CNAA developed (particularly those universities that were themselves engaged in various validation of degree programmes in the public sector), and many of the developments in the external examiner system referred to earlier in this chapter reflect the influence of the CNAA. But it is also true that the CNAA system was cumbersome, very time-consuming and often frustrating. More seriously, when supervision of standards is exercised through heavy and onerous written reporting procedures, there is a real danger that satisfaction of the paper requirements will be seen as ipso facto guaranteeing standards. The substance is lost in the form. The personal responsibility of the individual teacher is to a greater or lesser degree seen to be discharged by successful completion of the paperwork and by satisfying visiting groups; but the decisive determinant of academic standards is the personal skills, the personal standards, the professionalism, and the self-respect of the individual teacher. This was the guiding principle of the Lindop Report, '... the most reliable safeguard of standards is not external validation or any other outside control, it is the growth of the teaching institution as a self-critical academic community' (Lindop 1985). Governmental acceptance of the main recommendations of Lindop led to the CNAA progressively divesting itself of detailed control, by accrediting institutions to validate their own degree programmes (still for CNAA degrees), while retaining for itself an ultimate power of review.

These developments, first in the new universities, and subsequently in the operation of the CNAA, demonstrate the widespread opinion that monitoring by an external body is necessary in the early stages of a higher education institution; but that when, and only when, it has developed appropriate procedures and appointed staff able to create and share in an institutional ethos of professionalism and self-imposed high standards, detailed control by an external body is not only unnecessary but can be positively harmful This is not to deny any role at all to the CVCP Academic Audit Unit or the CNAA: both can valuably act to stimulate or develop improved procedures, to disseminate information about them, and to visit institutions from time to time for consultation and discussion. They should be composed in the main of high-ranking members of the academic profession, although members of industry and other professions concerned with higher education and training could add valuable counsel. HMI would seem not best-qualified to act in this way.

Conclusion
The discussion suggests the following conclusions. First, the external examiner system has little to offer in relation to the academic standards of the higher education system or of individual institutions within it. The purposes, and so the quality and standards, of the system are to be judged in the national context (one may note regret, in passing, at the government's rejection of the Croham Committee's recommendation for the establishment of an advisory Education Commission to co-ordinate the interests of various government departments involved with education, and to advise on objectives for the different parts of the higher education system). As far as institutions are concerned their quality and standards are to be judged in relation to the educational purposes of the whole institution: this may have social, physical,

broadly cultural, aesthetic, or spiritual as well as intellectual components; and external examiners relate only to the last of these, and perhaps only to part of that if degree programmes are mixed in a variety of ways. Nonetheless regular good reports from a majority of external examiners will provide good reason for confidence about the academic standards of an institution.

At the course or degree programme level quality and standards, in relation to the purposes of the course or programme, are decisively influenced by the skills, the professionalism, the self-imposed standards of the individual teacher. Of course consistently high performance will not be maintained by all teachers over their forty-year teaching lives without the assistance of some system of rewards and penalties, and that necessitates some monitoring procedures. The crucial requirement for monitoring procedures is that they serve to fortify rather than to substitute for the personal sense of responsibility of the individual teacher. The external examiner system, as it used to be operated, had small relevance to academic standards, properly defined. Within the context of other procedures that have recently been developed however, and with the enhanced and more clearly defined role of the external examiners themselves, it is my judgement that the system, if well operated in an encouraging and stimulating as well as critical way, can make the biggest single contribution to the maintenance and improvement of academic standards. The present tragedy is that governmental policies in the last three or four years would appear almost deliberately designed to undermine professionalism and the self-respect of the individual teacher. In such circumstances as these academic standards must inevitably decline.

References

Croham Committee (1987) Review of the University Grants Committee. (Cmnd 81) London: HMSO.

Lindop, Sir N. (Chairman) (1985) *Academic validation in public sector higher education report of the Committee of Enquiry into the academic validation of degree courses in public higher education.* (Cmnd 9501), para 7.4. London: HMSO.

Chapter Four
The Current Role of the Council for National Academic Awards
Richard Lewis

Every so often an aging and rather tired looking senior engineer or manager currently employed in industry turns up for a job interview at a polytechnic who, when asked why he or she has applied for a job, replies 'because I want to work in a more stable environment'. Fortunately for the sake of both the candidate and the polytechnic they rarely get the job because if they did the last thing they would find is stability. The point of this remark is not to suggest that life in industry is not hard but simply that higher education, and in particular the polytechnic and college sector, has experienced, is experiencing and will experience changes of a substantial order not always appreciated by those outside academia.

The CNAA has for the last 25 years had a major influence on the pace and direction of these developments. From time to time, it might have impeded progress but on the whole its contributions have been positive and it would take a foolhardy man or woman to assert that the quite outstanding success achieved by the polytechnic and college sector of higher education was not in part due to the existence of the Council for National Academic Awards.

The current role of the CNAA
However we live in changing times and cannot rest on past glories. What is the current role of the CNAA? An associated question is 'what should be the current role of the CNAA?'. The latter question is currently being reviewed by the Department of Education and Science (DES). The reaction of the government to this review will have a significant effect not only on the CNAA but on higher education in general.

The Council has always had two main roles, to award degrees (and other academic qualifications) and to sustain and enhance quality. In the past these two functions were seen as being intertwined but it is now being recognized, that whilst both these functions are related, they are distinct. It would be possible to be a degree awarding body and not be concerned with quality, or a quality assurance body which does not award degrees. The first, whilst possible, would clearly not be advisable but the second is both possible and may well, under the right conditions, be sensible.

Before proceeding to discuss the extent to which these two objectives might be disentangled it is helpful, by way of contextual background, to indicate the scale of the CNAA's activities as an awarding body. In the academic year 1988/89 some 240,000 students were registered on taught courses leading to a CNAA award and over 4000 students were following programmes of research leading to either the MPhil or PhD (CNAA, 1990 [a]). It is estimated that just over one-third of undergraduates studying in the UK are on CNAA courses and that there are now about 600,000 CNAA graduates, or about one per cent of the total population of the UK. The Council's role in this area is thus important in both quantitative as well qualitative terms.

The Education Reform Act
Two major changes, one gradual and one sudden, have influenced the Council's view of its role as the degree awarding body. The gradual change is the increasing academic maturity of the institutions offering CNAA awards. The sudden change was the incorporation of the English polytechnics and many of the English colleges as independent higher education corporations as a result of the Education Reform Act of 1988.

The phrase 'academic maturity' is worthy of some comment. Numerically it can be easily defended. All the polytechnics and many of the major colleges associated with the Council have been teaching at degree level for at least the 25 year life of the CNAA, with a good number of them having a much longer experience of work at this level through their involvement for example with external degrees, and in some cases internal degrees, of the University of London. However, maturity is not of itself an overriding virtue. It may, as in the case of a cheese, merely donate age and a strong odour. What is relevant is that age and experience have helped contribute to the creation of what the Council has termed 'self-critical academic communities' and it is the recognition that many institutions have now established themselves as such communities which has influenced the development of the Council's role both in its degree awarding and quality assurance functions. Not all CNAA related institutions are mature. The ever changing nature of higher education is such that new institutions, many of which are in some respect or other 'non-traditional', are coming forward wishing to offer courses leading to the Council's awards and the Council's role in respect of these organizations will be considered later in this chapter.

The constitutional change whereby many English institutions achieved independence is of considerable significance to the Council's role as a degree awarding body. Before 1 April 1989 the polytechnics and colleges in England had no separate legal status. They were, with some exceptions, owned as well as maintained by their local authorities. The establishment of the higher education corporations has allowed the Council to consider areas of further delegation of its powers to institutions which would not have been possible had they remained within the local government sector.

The CNAA 'Clause 3'

The recognition of the academic maturity of many of its associated institutions led to the Council petitioning for amendments to its charter and statutes which were granted by the Privy Council in 1987. Whilst at that time the radical nature of the Education Reform Act 1988 was not foreseen, the changes also facilitated the Council's response to the new circumstances created by the 1988 legislation. The Council's revised charter contains two significant clauses. Clause 3 (b) provides that the Council has the power:

> To permit such bodies as the Council may determine to act on its behalf in the conferment of degrees, diplomas, certificates and other academic awards and distinctions on persons who shall have either pursued approved courses of study or carried our approved programmes of supervised research and passed such examinations or other tests as may be required upon such terms and conditions as may from time to time be determined by the Council.

Whilst Clause 3 (c) allows the Council:

> To permit such bodies as the Council may from time to time determine, upon such terms and conditions and in relation to such cases as may be specified, to approve either courses of study or programmes of supervised research to be pursued by candidates to qualify for awards under this Our Charter.

Clause 3 (c) is about the approval of courses and relates to the Council's role as a quality assurance body. It has been activated through the 'accreditation' of certain institutions, of which more below.

Clause 3 (b) is about the conferment of degrees and other awards. At its meeting on 11 April 1990 the Council agreed that Clause 3 (b) should be implemented and invited applications from institutions which were both accredited, ie had been granted powers under Clause 3 (c), and incorporated.

In some respects the delegation of the power to confer awards might be regarded as mechanistic, which is not to suggest that it is trivial. Under existing arrangements the Council has to approve the validity of the pass list issued by boards of examiners before the degree can be awarded. Under 3 (b) this task would be undertaken by the institution. In other respects the change is very significant because it exposes the question of whose degree is it? Is it a degree of the CNAA gained following a course of studies at 'Loamshire Polytechnic' or is it a degree of 'Loamshire Polytechnic' awarded under the powers of the charter of the CNAA? The latter interpretation is the more apt and the changes currently being introduced will help establish this point in the public mind.

Important as all this is, the critical issue is the standard of the award or to put it more fully, the quality of the student's experience in higher education, the reliability of the award achieved by the graduate as a measure of his or her abilities as judged against the objectives of the course and issues concerned with consistency across the higher education sector.

For the benefit of those who are unaware of the procedures of the CNAA it might be helpful to provide a brief, inevitably over simplified, description of the way in which the Council operated before the implementation of Clause 3 (c).

In order to obtain the Council's approval for a course leading to an award the institution had to go through two stages. It had to be approved as providing a suitable environment for courses leading to the Council's awards. This involved an initial application which would include a site visit by academic peers and reapproval every five years. Reapproval being based on the institution's own critical appraisal of its progress over the quinquennium which would be discussed in the course of a site visit.

Approval of individual courses followed a similar path. An institution would, through documentation, propose a programme of study and, if a prima facie case was made, the institution would be visited by a team of specialists drawn from one of the Council's 40 or so subject boards. Courses were reviewed every five years based on documentation produced by institutions which would review progress and proposed changes. Reapproval largely depended on the dialogue between the course team and the representatives of the appropriate subject board. Over the years, even before the implementation of Clause 3 (c), the approach had been modified most significantly to introduce elements of partnership which allowed institutions to take a greater role in the organization of the approval and reapproval of events and to permit representatives of the institution, independent of the course being reviewed, to become members of the 'visiting party'.

Thus whilst accreditation represents a significant change in the 'balance of power' between the institution and the Council it can nonetheless be viewed as a logical development of the Council's approach to quality assurance. The first institutions were accredited in April 1988 and by April 1990 some 38 institutions are in accreditation. Whilst the number of accredited institutions, which include all the polytechnics, still represent a minority of the 130 or so institutions which use the Council's charter, it is estimated that about 85 per cent of students on CNAA courses are to be found in accredited institutions.

Accreditation procedures
In these comparatively early days of accreditation many institutions still base their own procedures on those of the Council but changes are being made in particular in respect of periodical (five year) reviews of courses. Some institutions are extending the process to allow more interaction between the reviewers and the course team, sometimes involving observation of the 'course in action'.

One feature of the CNAA approach which does persist is the use of external specialists in the approval and reapproval of courses as it is a condition of accreditation that at least two externals, including someone with current industrial professional experience, should be involved in this work. Changes in the ways in which courses are reviewed following accreditation are being monitored by both the Council and HMI and are the subject of two recent reports (CNAA (1990 [b]) and HMI (1990)).

When considering an institution's application for accreditation the Council looks at its 'total approach' to quality assurance. Accreditation is gained by the submission of a document which is followed by a visit from a relatively small number of academic peers, albeit, especially in the first phase of accreditation, peers with considerable experience and seniority. In assessing an application the Council does not seek to approve the institution's existing arrangements for quality assurance. However, the Council does seek to assure itself that there is an ethos in the institution which fosters quality assurance. In particular, the accredited institution has to show how quality assurance permeates the life of the institution including the day to day management of courses and the annual monitoring and evaluation of performance. The evidence is that accredited institutions have accepted their enhanced responsibilities with vigour and enthusiasm.

Another change brought about by accreditation, but foreshadowed by the partnership agreements which proceeded it, is the broadening of the membership of the 'visiting parties', to continue to use the useful, albeit partially obsolete, title. Traditionally, the academic peer group reviewing a course was drawn from the discipline concerned but now members are drawn from a wider range of subjects. Whilst this can create a risk, which should not be overlooked, that certain technical aspects of the curriculum may not receive due attention, it has meant that broader pedagogic issues are given greater attention and does allow certain discipline-based assumptions about the nature of higher education to be challenged.

The changes I have described thus far indicate the Council has moved away from the approval of courses to that of ensuring that institutions have themselves the means and the will to carry out this function. But the Council believes that its role in quality assurance must go beyond this. The foundation of peer group evaluation would be insecure if it relied entirely on the knowledge and experience of a relatively small group of people. The experience of individuals is bound to be idiosyncratic and partial; the possibility of any one individual having an extensive overview of all developments in a field will be even more unlikely as higher education expands to satisfy the needs of the 21st century. In the past, individual members of visiting parties could draw on the collective wisdom of the subject boards of which they were members. These subject boards were stood down as part of the Council's policy of devolving responsibility to institutions but the Council felt it necessary to replace that collective wisdom by other means which would help the judgemental operation which inevitably underlies the review of courses. These developments which are regarded as an essential part of the Council's new role in quality assurance, and not an optional extra, are entirely consonant with the Council's traditional role of seeking to disseminate best practice.

To this end the Council has initiated a number of developments including:

1. The CNAA Digest.
This is published three times a year and contains information which is of value to those who design and operate courses as well as those who review them. The publication has been well received by those for whom it is intended; a particularly valuable resource of the Council is its mailing list for it is able to send a copy of the Digest to all CNAA course leaders.

2. A rolling programme of subject and course development.
This programme has just started and was, perhaps because of uncertainties about its nature, treated with some suspicion in one or two quarters who believed that it might seek to replicate the 'old CNAA'. This is not the case. These reviews seek to identify important development in the teaching and learning of subjects to provide benchmarks against which particular schemes can be judged. Whilst an important element of the review is an identification of current developments their potential will only be fully realized if they look to the future. Industrialists, practitioners and employers also need to be involved so that the reviews can indicate ways in which courses might develop to respond to changes in needs. The value of the exercise has been evidenced by the fact that industrial sponsorship has been obtained which has allowed the programme to be advanced at a more rapid pace than reliance on the Council's recourses would have allowed. It is the intention to cover each major field of activity every four years or so.

3. Student database.
The student database is a secondary database and does not involve institutions in supplying data over and above existing requirements. The database does, however, have a unique facility in being able to allow investigations of relationships between output performance and input characteristics. It also provides information about, for example, final degree classifications and graduate destinations which provide benchmarks against which institutions can judge the performance of their students and graduates. Its use is being developed in close association with a number of institutions and it is already being employed extensively by a number of polytechnics and colleges in their course reviews.

4. A register of specialist advisers.

The Council maintains and publishes a register of some 1500 specialist advisers including academics (from both the polytechnic and college and university sectors), industrialists and practitioners who assist the Council in the review of courses in non-accredited (or associated) institutions and in the approval of external examiners. (The Council believes that it is important to continue to have the right to approve the appointment of all external examiners including those concerned with courses in accredited institutions.) The register is also used by accredited institutions to identify people who can be asked to assist in course reviews.

5. Workshops and conferences.

The Council has established a successful programme of workshops and conferences which relate directly to the needs of quality assurance. Recent workshops have dealt with such subjects as examining, the use of the student database and meetings of members of the register of specialist advisers.

Credit Accumulation and Transfer Scheme (CATS)

Other dimensions of the Council's involvement in quality assurance include the credit accumulation and transfer scheme (CATS) and its involvement with the national scheme for the recognition of access courses.

CATS was established in 1986 and exists to increase opportunities in higher education. The establishment of a tariff scheme which has been adopted by many polytechnics, colleges and universities as well as regional consortia, help students transfer from one institution to another with appropriate academic credit which can be applied against an approved programme of study. In addition students can, but always in the context of an approved programme of study, obtain a qualification from credits derived from a number of sources which might include learning obtained in employment as well as in traditional institutions of higher education.

A related activity has been the credit rating of employment based courses and the credit rating of certain professional qualifications. Most of this work has been carried out by institutions and has resulted in a good deal of collaborative activity involving employers and higher education. Although the operation has been centred on the CNAA, CATS is in many respects a transbinary operation and a number of formal and informal agreements have been made between the Council and universities which facilitate student transfer.

Access to higher education

Another recent development with a strong transbinary flavour is the
Council's involvement in the establishment of a national framework
for the recognition of access courses for entry to higher education. This
was established by the Council in partnership with the Committee of
Vice Chancellors and Principals (CVCP) in 1989 at the request of the
DES. The central group the Access Courses Recognition Group,
which reports both to the CNAA and CVCP, approves local agencies
which may be universities, CNAA related institutions or a consortium
involving universities or CNAA institutions which themselves validate
access courses. By April 1990 twenty-two validating agencies had been
approved and eighteen applications were under consideration.

Conclusion

The frontiers of higher education are not fixed. Higher education takes
place in industry and commerce, in charitable and religious establishments and in government. The flexibility of the Council allows it to
respond to requests from a very wide range of organizations who wish
to be able to offer CNAA awards. Some of these initiatives, such as in
the Health Service, involve large numbers of people and are mainly in
response to the need to improve the standard of qualifications of
important professional and occupational groups which have hitherto
fallen outside the HE sector. In other cases the number of students
involved is very small but the ability to be able to take courses leading
to CNAA awards allows new ideas to be tried, many of which will have
a major impact on the mainstream of higher education.

In such a fast changing world as higher education to write a chapter
on the current role of anything risks producing something more
obsolete than the Blue Streak, or even Stephenson's Rocket.
However, it is clear that despite the changes that have taken place in
the operations of the Council for National Academic Awards its
overriding concern with quality continues as does its desire to facilitate
the response of higher education to the changing needs of the country?

A theme common to the old, current and existing CNAA is the need
to balance innovation with quality. Too rigid an adherence to
outmoded views of quality will inhibit change. At the same time a too
rapid introduction of change without concerns of quality will produce a
product not worth having. The success of the Council will be judged by
the extent to which it has helped higher education to find a balance
between these extremes.

References

CNAA (1990 [a]) *CNAA Annual Report for 1988–89*.

CNAA (1990 [b]) *Changing Patterns of Course Review*.

HMI (1990) *A Survey of Validation and Review. Arrangements of CNAA Courses*. DES (Ref 58/90/NS).

Chapter Five
The Introduction of Staff Appraisal in Universities as a Method of Quality Assurance
Cari Loder

The accountability movement of the 1970s, coupled with government policy and the financial management initiative throughout the public domain in the early 1980s, and the cuts of 1981, has brought the question of appraisal into the public arena. Prior to this the issue had never seriously been considered for academic staff. In 1984 the UGC in their document *A strategy for higher education into the 1990s* stated:

> Staff appraisal has become much more searching and constructive for professional staff in many organisations. In the universities there are modest staff development programmes and some systematic induction for new staff is now common. This is not enough.

A year later the Jarratt Report (1985) was more explicit:

> Universities are unusual in that little formal attempt is made on a regular basis to appraise academic staff with a view to their personal development and to successful planning within the institution. We believe this to be of crucial importance ... A regular review procedure, handled with sensitivity, would be of benefit to staff, and to the university as a whole.

The Jarratt Report identified in some detail what it considered to be the objectives of appraisal:

> In considering the form of staff appraisal system for a university, three main objectives can be identified:
> a) Recognition of the contribution made by individuals.
> b) Assistance for individuals to develop their full potential as quickly as possible
> c) Assistance for the university to make the most effective use of its academic staff.
> We recommend an annual review on this basis as is the practice in the best staff development systems used elsewhere.

The situation in the polytechnic and college sector is slightly different in that more attention has been devoted to an evaluation of staffing levels than in the universities, largely due to their involvement in CNAA validation procedures, which examined institutional resources of which staff development are a prime element.

However, even the CNAA has been criticized for concentrating more on formal qualifications and possible research output and consultancies undertaken by staff, than on teaching.

In 1987 the CVCP and AUT produced a joint document on career development and staff appraisal procedures for academic and academic-related staff (CVCP 1987). The covering note pointed out the difference in approach between the parties. The CVCP sees appraisal as 'a way of significantly improving the quality of information about staff performance available to management; as a means of identifying improvements in organization; and as a way to improve staff performance. AUT representatives view the process as primarily concerned with professional self-development.'

What is appraisal?
Appraisal has been defined as a process of assessing an individual's performance over a period of time against defined criteria of acceptable performance. This definition of staff appraisal implies that two things can be achieved: that it is possible to establish performance criteria for a given post and that individual staff performance can be measured against these criteria.

However, there is a serious tension between viewing appraisal as a means of improving performance (formative) and as a method of judging performance (summative), even if some argue that these two purposes do not necessarily have to be mutually exclusive.

There does seem to be general agreement with Nuttall (1986), however who states categorically that:

> An effective scheme cannot serve formative and summative purposes simultaneously ... experience from the USA shows that in a dual-purpose scheme summative considerations usually prevail, resulting in negligible teacher improvement.

It is perhaps inevitable that forming judgements about staff performance will be seen as an easier task than attempting to identify and implement ways of improving performance which requires a commitment on the part of both the individual and the institution.

It is considered self-evident that staff who are concerned about their performance will obviously want to know they are doing a good professional job and will therefore welcome feedback, help and support in improving their knowledge and skills. In that sense a system of staff appraisal is likely to be welcomed by all committed practitioners in academia. Andreson and Powell (1986) see evaluation of performance as an integral part of the academic ethos:

> Academics are professionals and must therefore be deeply concerned about the ways in which they conduct their daily work and the manner in which competence in its conduct ought to be determined. Evaluation lies at the heart of academic life because learning, scholarship and research could not advance in its absence...

This rather idealized picture of academics might possibly have a stronger purchase on reality if staff appraisal was solely concerned with improving professional conduct but as Nisbet points out staff appraisal has three main functions of teacher appraisal

Standards   ie to maintain and improve teaching and learning

Accountability   ie to reinforce a sense of responsibility and allay possible public misgiving

Management   ie to raise the quality of performance to cope with change and aid in decision making

It is unlikely that many academic staff would find reason to object to the above aims. Indeed, many staff would welcome the opportunity for further personal development. However, there is currently a great deal of unease about the introduction of a university-wide appraisal programme. Uncertainty about the purpose of staff appraisal, lack of motivation on the part of staff to participate in appraisal, institutional difficulties with implementing effective appraisal systems (selecting appropriate appraisers, providing resources for training appraisers and providing effective staff development etc) all serve to undermine enthusiasm for what should have been a well-received innovation.

There are also questions and a good deal of scepticism about the effectiveness and efficiency of staff appraisal as a means of improving the quality of teaching and research in higher education.

Appraisal of individual teacher performance
The literature on the appraisal of teaching staff is extensive and in many cases borrows from and builds on both organizational studies literature on appraisal and on analysis of schemes currently in use in

commercial companies and other public services. These texts make a clear and fundamental distinction between appraisal for staff development and improvement (formative) and appraisal for promotion and other rewards (summative).

In the United States faculty evaluation has become a major industry but is perhaps guilty of having become too tightly focussed on appraisal for the purpose of selection, tenure and promotion; it has been too reliant on a single instrument, the student questionnaire, to rate faculty. Teaching has been given too little weight in staff evaluation in relation to research. In too many schemes teachers are the objects of, rather than participants in, the evaluation process and this reduces the potential for improvement in teaching and learning through evaluation.

The Australian literature on staff appraisal is particularly interesting because it draws on work done both in North America and the United Kingdom, and because it has been written in a political/policy context which has a number of striking similarities with the situation in the UK. The Commonwealth Tertiary Education Commission's 1986 review of efficiency and effectiveness in tertiary education concluded that:

> the only reliable and effective approach is a formal system of staff assessment and it is only in this way that the institution can demonstrate that it is exercising its obligation to ensure the effective use of public funds within a tenure system. The [assessment] schemes should be designed to assist staff to monitor their performance and provide feedback on how they may develop strength and overcome weaknesses, as well as to provide assistance to the institution in its decision-making provision.

In is undoubtedly true that teachers fill a number of different roles, work in a variety of situations in which they often do not control important contextual variables, teach different subjects with different imperatives where 'knowing that' (information), 'knowing how' (skills) and 'knowing why' (understanding) may be more or less important, and often have a fairly consistent disposition towards a particular style of teaching. All these factors should be taken into account when appraising teachers.

Although there is no one definition of effective teaching, there is, however, some research that suggests the characteristics of the effective teacher can be defined as:

- mastery of subject matter
- concern for students

- stimulation of student interest
- clarity of explanation
- enthusiasm for the subject
- encouragement of student participation
- availability for student consultation
- fairness in grading
- preparation and organization
- public speaking ability
- ability to stimulate independent learning

Peer review can play an important part in the appraisal process, particularly in relation to:

- academic quality of course
- quality and substance of course teaching materials
- quality of students' work including examination scripts and thesis
- contribution to the academic vitality of the course team/department

It is important to note that the role of colleagues in formative evaluation, particularly their effectiveness as consultants in the process of teaching improvement, has not yet been validated in relation to student outcomes. However, Cross (1987) maintains that teachers can derive considerable benefit from working with colleagues on teaching issues and outlines several areas where peer evaluation can be profitably employed.

It is suggested that teachers themselves can evaluate:

- materials prepared for teaching
- teaching skills in a variety of settings, eg lectures, seminars, tutorials, fieldwork, post-graduate supervision
- teaching innovations
- examination methods used
- evaluation techniques adopted

However, no matter how effectively peer review of teaching is employed, I would claim that an appraisal system can not obtain all relevant information without eliciting student feedback on the teaching and learning process.

The use of student feedback

There is also a wide literature, again mainly American, on the part feedback from students can play in the assessment of teaching quality. Some studies have found that when student instructional ratings were used for administrative personnel decisions, some faculty members raised grades and lowered academic standards in an attempt to win favourable evaluations from students, but this seems to be the exception rather than the rule.

Cross (1987), after reviewing the literature concludes that, although the findings are sufficiently positive to suggest student questionnaires are *one* important source of feedback for the improvement of teaching, their use would be improved if students were taught to be careful observers of the impact of teaching on their learning; if teachers were allowed to design questions specific to their teaching objectives and the course they are teaching; and if the feedback to teachers was augmented by conversation with someone with expert knowledge on teaching and learning. There are also problems about the use made of student evaluations. One study found that lecturing commitments were much reduced as a result of poor student evaluations.

Whether or not staff are evaluated formally or informally, and whether or not the purpose is formative or summative (or a combination of the two) student questionnaires almost invariably play a significant part in the evaluation. Like the wider literature on staff evaluation, that which is restricted to the reliability, validity and effectiveness of student questionnaires is extensive, and not surprisingly, given the ubiquitous use of the questionnaire in the United States to rank non-tenured faculty, is dominated by the Americans.

Murray (1984) comes to the conclusion that although the research results on students rating questionnaires are complex and sometimes contradictory:

> most writers have concluded that student ratings of teaching are sufficiently reliable and valid to justify their use both for diagnostic feedback to instructors and as one of several sources of information in administrative decisions on faculty salary, retentions, tenure and promotion

However, others have suggested that one of the major concerns associated with student evaluation of teaching is the extent to which such a procedure is valid. Student evaluations have been shown to be reliable but the question of their validity is less clear. It can be argued that it is reasonable to judge the quality of teaching by assessing the students' learning outcomes. However, 'the relationship between student learning and the quality of teaching (no matter how defined) is not a simple one'. (Jones 1989)

Survey instruments for obtaining student views on their teachers have been improved over the years. If asked appropriate questions students have been found to be the best judges of a) teaching methods; b) fairness; c) interest in students; d) interest in subject and e) global questions, eg comparative information. (Kogan 1989)

Another major issue is when student evaluations of staff and courses are conducted. There is evidence that most academic staff gather their students evaluations towards the end of the academic year (often when it is too late to do anything about the concerns of the students), but Seldin (1988) reports that some professors gather mid-term ratings so that areas of student dissatisfaction (and satisfaction) can be addressed in the second half.

Even when well-designed questionnaires are administered at appropriate intervals it has been found that the use of student ratings do not automatically result in improved teaching. Improvement appears to be dependent on three factors: whether the ratings are new to the lecturer; whether he is motivated to improve; and whether he knows how to improve. Murray and Newby (1982) at the University of Western Ontario found that only 54 per cent of faculty respondents stated that student evaluation had provided useful feedback for improvement of teaching.

Renner (1986) found that the use of student instructional ratings for administrative personnel decisions resulted in some faculty members raising grades and lowering academic standards in an attempt to 'buy' favourable evaluations from students and Ryan *et al* (1980) found that instructors at the University of Wisconsin Lacrosse reported significant increases in a number of practices that would usually be viewed as good teaching, but also increased use of undesirable teaching behaviours, for example, smoothing the path of students, and so on balance they felt teaching was not overall improved.

It has been suggested that student feedback is only an effective stimulus for the improvement of teaching if it is supplemented by expert consultation, in which case it was found that instructor ratings at the end of the course were higher, and that students also had higher class means on a common final examination and on measure of student motivation. Even where staff have positive attitudes towards student evaluation of teaching, they still felt that it was threatening and found consultation of importance. However, student ratings undeniably have their limitations, they can provide only limited information on certain aspects of teaching and performance and in most cases must be supplemented by other sources of judgement.

The relationship between teaching and research
Although there appears to be no conclusive evidence of a positive correlation between teaching effectiveness and research, Perry (1987) maintains that good teaching can properly be described as 'appropriate for undergraduate and postgraduate students must be enlivened by the lecturer's own research and scholarly pursuits, and must share with students the lecturer's constantly renewed thinking about the subject and its methodology.'

Ball (1988) takes much the same position on the relation between teaching and research arguing that the pursuit of advanced study must be recognized and funded as a part of the teaching function. Others have commented that at one extreme academics are researchers concerned with the advancement of knowledge, and at the other extreme they are teachers who are aware and can draw on research in what they teach. It is pointed out that the relation between research and teaching changes from one discipline to another and at different stages in an academic's life. The precise role of research in 'teaching-first' institutions is difficult to determine, but since it is clearly recognized as a necessary activity in PCFC funded institutions, it should be appraised in formative as well as summative evaluation.

Appraisal and institutional management
Some commentators argue that evaluation for staff development and the improvement of teaching should be kept strictly separate whereas others think there are ways they can be combined. However, all seem to agree that if formative evaluation is going to work it must be related to the institution's reward system. Murray (1984) points out:

> Surveys of faculty opinion indicate that, despite reservations about certain aspects of teaching evaluation, most faculty members in North American universities believe that teaching should be given increased weight in salary, promotion and tenure decisions. It is unreasonable to expect the faculty members to put time and effort into the improvement of teaching if their accomplishments in this area go unrecognized in the institutional reward system.

There are several reasons for linking appraisal schemes to the institutional reward structure:

- it more properly reflects the importance of teaching in the contractual, professional and operational responsibility of the staff
- it restores the status and credibility of teaching in the attitudes and practices of the staff

- it provides a clear means of recognizing and rewarding professional merit in teaching
- it provides tangible incentives to staff for the time and effort needed to bring about improved teaching performance
- it provides a means of quality control for teaching.

The criteria for a successful and positive system of staff appraisal has been suggested as being one which facilitates an ethos of institutional self-evaluation and constructive self-criticism, a positive climate amongst staff, a good professional self-image, high morale and a commitment to appraisal and to acting upon its results. It is essential that appraisal lead to appropriate action and that all those who are to be appraised should be involved in the process at all stages and that any appraisal should leave the appraisee a measure of autonomy.

However, appropriate action can be a problem in that although it is possible to identify members of staff whose teaching is obviously unsatisfactory, implementing positive action to remedy the situation is much more difficult.

The issue at present is not whether staff appraisal per se is a valid method of quality assurance, as universities have no choice but to put appraisal into practice, but rather how appraisal schemes can be judged to be adequate and appropriate. An effective staff appraisal scheme must address the needs of the appraisee, the needs of the department, and the aims and requirements of the institutions. A staff appraisal programme which deals effectively with the personal development needs of an individual, but does not address the relevance of these needs to the institution as a whole, is not going to prove an effective means of assuring quality within the particular institution. It is therefore essential that the underlying aims of introducing a programme of staff appraisal are clearly defined. Even assuming that appraisal aims are defined and clearly addressed, that the personal and professional development needs of those being appraised are being met, and that staff at all levels are committed to a programme of appraisal, the system will be ineffective unless sufficient resources are made available by the institution to train appraisers to a high standard and to provide the means by which problems that are identified via appraisal can be remedied via a well-structured, relevant on-going programme of staff development.

It is already apparent that many universities are introducing staff appraisal programmes merely because they are required to do so by the CVCP. This imposition of appraisal is resulting, in the worst cases, in universities preparing an appraisal programme that adheres to the letter of the requirement but reflects none of the spirit. Effective programmes require commitment at all levels of participants from the Director or Vice Chancellor of the university to the research officer employed on a fixed term contract. If appraisal is perceived at any level as being at best an innocuous irritation, and at worst a threat to professional autonomy it is doomed to failure from the start. However, the picture is not as gloomy as it is being painted.

Many universities have welcomed the chance to provide a peer review form of assessment and support for their staff, and are implementing well-developed and highly constructive appraisal programmes. It is not surprising that in those institutions that have a history of a commitment to staff development, the appraisal procedures tend to be focussed on individual professional development. It is not yet known to what extent those who are to be appraised have been involved in the development of appraisal programmes in universities, but there is some evidence to support the belief that it is the more senior tenured staff who have been making decisions about how to appraise those with a far less secure position within academia.

There has been much discussion about who should undertake the work of appraisal; 'It is essential that appraisers have the confidence of the appraisees. For this reason, they should be experienced and responsible members of staff who have been formally recognized by the institution as appraisers and who have been properly trained for, and have sufficient time to devote to, their appraisal duties.' (CVCP 1987 paragraph 4a)

More specifically Nisbet (1986) suggests the following options for staff appraisal:

a) leave staff appraisal to heads of departments and keep it an internal private matter;
b) design a self-appraisal procedure for departments or for whole institutions or for individuals so that standards can be discussed more openly, but still privately within the institution;
c) wrap up the appraisal procedure in a positively worded programme of 'staff development' in which planning ahead is discussed as well as assessing past performance, thus minimizing the implicit threat – though in some appraisal schemes the wrapping of 'staff development' only thinly covers a strong element of compulsion and authoritative scrutiny.

The issue of confidentiality is one that will become of increasing importance as staff appraisal is put into practice across the sector. It is undoubtedly true that those institutions which chose to review the outcome of appraisal interviews to the personnel office may well find the appraisees unwilling to talk frankly about their needs and concerns. However, institutions who chose to keep information totally confidential between the appraiser and the appraisee may equally find that the event is taken far less seriously than would be desired.

It appears that the majority of appraisal programmes will be based on a system of interviews between appointed appraisers and appraisees. However, if appraisal is to be used seriously as a means of quality assurance then I believe that opinions and judgements must be sought not only from the appraiser and the individual themselves but from students and other professional colleagues.

It is acknowledged that each of these contributors have positive attributes:

> no more reliable index exists than ... 'peer review' ... This is not to say that there is no room for improvement in the manner in which peer review is carried out, or that it is a strong enough reed to carry all the burdens that might be thrust upon it ... It is only to say that peer review is tried and tested and is the best way we have of evaluating quality in higher education. (Moodie 1986)

But it is also important to note that there are also negative attributes:

> Peer review and expert judgement are inevitably the main procedures for assessing most aspects of performance in higher education. They have the advantages of relevance, flexibility and the internalization of standards being evaluated. There are, however, dangers: they encourage conventionality and discourage innovation.' (Williams 1986)

A final warning is provided by Rutherford (1988) and is echoed by Moses (1989):

> The scheme will involve a great deal of work for those academics who, having been chosen for senior positions by dint of their academic work are already almost prevented from pursuing that work by the flood of paperwork, the endless committee meetings and the like! This will simply add to that, not only from the internal university assessments but also, no doubt, heads of departments and other senior academics will be asked to comment on the performance of other departments in other institutions.

References

Andreson, L.W. and Powell, J.P. (1987) Competent teaching and its appraisal. *Assessment and evaluation in higher education*, 12/1, Spring, pp.66–72.

Ball, C. (1988) Keynote Speech. *In* Eggins, H. (ed) *Restructuring Higher Education: Proceedings of Annual Conference* pp.3–12 Milton Keynes: SRHE/Open University Press.

Cross, K.P. (1987) *Feedback In The Classroom: making assessment matter*. Assessment Forum, American Association for Higher Education.

CVCP (1986) *Performance indicators in universities: a first statement by a joint CVCP/UGC working group*. London: CVCP, July.

CVCP (1987) *Career development and staff appraisal procedures for academic and academic related staff* (CVCP and AUT joint document). London: CVCP, November.

CVCP (1987b) *Appraisal, promotion procedures and probation: note to Vice Chancellors and Principals* (N87/108). London: CVCP, 2nd December.

Jarratt, A. (Chairman) (1985) *Report of the Steering Committee for Efficiency Studies in Universities*. London: CVCP.

Jones, J. (1989) Students' ratings of teacher personality and teaching competence. *Higher education*, 18, pp.551–8.

Kogan, M. (ed) (1989) *Evaluating higher education*. London: Jessica Kingsley.

Moodie, G.C. (1986) Fit for what? *In* G.C. Moodie (ed) *Standards and criteria in higher education*. Guildford: SRHE & NFER/Nelson.

Moses, I. (1985b) High quality teaching in a university: identification and description. *Studies in higher education*, 10/3, pp.301–313.

Moses, I. (1989) Role and problems of heads of departments in performance appraisal. *Assessment and evaluation in higher education*, 14/2, Summer, pp.95–105.

Murray, H.G. (1984) The impact of formative and summative evaluation of teaching in North American universities. *Assessment and evaluation in higher education*, 9/2, Summer, pp.117–32.

Murray, H.G. and Newby, W.G. (1982) Faculty attitudes towards evaluation of teaching at the University of Western Ontario. *Assessment and evaluation in higher education*, 7/2, pp.144–51.

Nisbet, J. (1986a) Staff and standards. *In* G.C. Moodie (ed) *Standards and criteria in higher education*. Guildford: SRHE & NFER/Nelson, pp.90–106.

Nisbet, J. (1986b) Appraisal for improvement. *In* E. Stones and B. Wilcox (eds) *Appraising appraisal.* Birmingham: British Educational Research Association, pp.10–19.

Nuttall, D. (1986) What can we learn from research on teaching and appraisal? *In* E. Stones and B. Wilcox *Appraising appraisal.* Birmingham: British Educational Research Association, pp.20–28.

Perry, P. (1987) Accountability and Inspection in Higher Education. *Higher Education Quarterly* Vol. 41 No. 4, pp.344–353.

Renner, R.R. *et al* (1986) Responsible behaviour as effective teaching: a new look at student rating of professors. *Assessment and evaluation in higher education*, 11/2, pp.138–45.

Rutherford, D. (1988) Performance appraisal: a survey of academic staff opinion. *Studies in Higher Education*, 13/1, pp.89–100.

Ryan, J.J. *et al* (1980) Student evaluation: the faculty responds. *Research in higher education*, 12, pp.317–333.

Seldin, P. (1988) Evaluating college teaching. *New directions for teaching and learning*, 33, pp.47–56.

UGC (1984) *A strategy for higher education into the 1990s.* London: HMSO.

Williams, G. (1986) The missing bottom line. *In* G.C. Moodie (ed) *Standards and criteria in higher education.* Guildford: SRHE & NFER/Nelson.

Chapter Six
Strategic Change in the Higher Education Curriculum: the Example of the Enterprise in Higher Education Initiative
Peter Wright[1]

Reappraising the purpose and quality of HE in Europe

During the 1980s European higher education has been under great pressure to reconsider and to redefine its purpose. Financial stringency, calls for greater public accountability, and changes in the relationship between higher education, government and industry have each served as spurs towards reappraisal. But, at a deeper level, each of these factors has ultimately been driven by a process of fundamental transformation: the movement from an elite to a mass system of higher education.

Nowhere is this more apparent than in Britain, where it is now government policy to raise the higher education age-participation from 14.6 per cent in 1986 to just under 20 per cent by the year 2000 (DES 1987, p. 9); and where some, including the Council for Industry and Higher Education, have called for much greater increases of 30 per cent or more (CIHE 1987, p. 1). Recent changes in the funding of HE seem likely to fuel expansion by giving greater weight to fees, which will tend to motivate institutions to recruit more students.[2]

Growth will change the student clientele in two important ways. First, it will necessitate the admission of 18-year-olds who have not attained the two A-level passes which are the traditional, highly subject-specialized entry requirement for a degree course in England and Wales (but not in Scotland)[3]. That will be so because the number of traditionally qualified young people seems most unlikely to expand anything like fast enough to match the overall growth. The proportion of young people who study for A-levels is small and shows little sign of rapid growth. (At present, only around 15 per cent of the age group attain two, or more, A-level passes.) (DES 1988, Table 9). Second, it will require the recruitment of a disproportionately larger number of older students since the number of people aged 18 and 19 is falling. From 1982 to 1996, it will decline by 34 per cent in England and Wales. This fall will become steepest after 1991, when it will accelerate to roughly three times its speed in the late 1980s.[4]

A great deal of change has already taken place in British higher educational institutions in response to shifts in their environment, to a succession of new government policies and to new methods for allocating funds. Nonetheless, at least as far as the curriculum or pedagogy are concerned, changes have generally been gradual and reactive, usually taking the form of 'discipline-led incrementalism' (Boys *et al* 1988), rather than of deliberate strategic planning.

Thorough-going discussion of the future shape of British HE is only now just beginning to take place, particularly under the impact of the Royal Society of Arts' Higher Education for Capability consultations and the work of the Council for Industry and Higher Education. So far, however, it has still scarcely touched many parts of higher education, still less involved the majority of academics. (RSA 1990)

There is little sign of a general readiness to acknowledge the full significance of the changes described above, nor to consider what their impact might be on the conventional presuppositions underlying higher education.

Almost no public discussion has taken place on how the changing situation of higher education will affect central issues such as the subject matter and level of its courses, the definition of their intended outcomes, the styles of learning which should be encouraged, or the appropriate methods of assessment. There has been scant debate on whether a new, expanded higher education system would entail new criteria for judging quality.

And yet these topics would seem the necessary starting point for a re-evaluation of the work of British colleges, polytechnics and universities. If the system is to make itself accessible and attractive to a much wider – and more varied – section of the population than hitherto it seems inescapable that there will need to be a movement away from disciplinary specialization. Similarly, it also seems inevitable that there will have to be fundamental shifts towards student-centred styles of learning and towards the explicit definition of the objectives of courses in terms of general learning outcomes; and, in consequence, the creation of methods of assessment that measure their attainment. (For a fuller discussion of this argument see Wright [1988]).

Indeed, such changes are already well advanced in schools and further education colleges (I discuss these in more detail below) and are changing the expectations of even that tiny minority of young people who attain A-levels. Soon, they will impinge directly on higher education. In the autumn of 1990, for example, the first students with GCSE qualifications will begin to enter higher educational establishments.

Although there seems to be an overwhelming case that higher education should be undertaking wide-ranging curricular reappraisal and development to prepare itself for the radically new environment of the 1990s, there is little evidence, so far, of much progress.

Curricular development in British education
The absence of curricular development in higher education becomes all the more striking when it is contrasted with what has been happening in British schools and further education colleges. In these, the last five years have been a period of intense activity which has included, at least four major examples of curricular development.

The first is the reorganization of the public examination system for 16-year-olds, which has led to the setting up of the GCSE (General Certificate of Secondary Education) which deliberately places much greater emphasis on independent learning, and criterion-referenced assessment related to explicit learning outcomes. The second is the definition and enforcement of a National Curriculum which defines the common areas to be studied by all pupils and sets attainment targets for various age groups. The third is the piloting, and subsequent extension, of TVEI (the Technical and Vocational Education Initiative), a scheme to increase the relevance of 14–19 education to the world of work and to foster the general personal qualities of value in it. Finally, there is the work to review and update vocational qualifications, being undertaken by the NCVQ (National Council for Vocational Qualifications). This aims to establish a coherent national system of accredited vocational qualifications at defined levels. The components of which will have clear outcomes, expressed in terms of competence, that will have been agreed with relevant employers and will form the criteria for assessment.[5]

Despite obvious differences between these examples of curricular development, they have in common four important characteristics: each has been a self-consciously planned attempt at making educational provision more appropriate to changing circumstances; each has attempted to direct the educational process towards specified outcomes that are accessible to a wider audience than that of professional educationalists – in particular, to potential students and to employers;

each has attempted to promote active involvement and personal capability and, thus, to encourage students to take more responsibility for their own learning; each has involved some shift from norm-referenced to criterion-referenced assessment (that is, from grading the performance of students relative to one another to grading it against a set of detailed criteria of performance).

Although it is too soon to expect consensus on whether or not these initiatives have been successful in achieving their aims, there can no doubt that they have already brought about substantial changes in the curriculum and assessment of those between 14 and 19.

Collectively, they seem likely to bring about a major change in how quality is defined in 14–19 education – their common theme is to cast it in terms of skills and attributes that extend beyond the confines of academic subject-based specialization and are comprehensible to those who are themselves not professional educators.

Curricular change in British higher education

In contrast, there are few examples of planned curricular development in British higher education; certainly, none with the impact and scale of the four programmes mentioned above.

Those which have occurred have usually been the fruits of localized enthusiasm, and have failed to spread across the HE system as a whole. Into this category can be grouped various attempts at the promotion of broader, inter-disciplinary courses, such as that, in the late forties, of the University College of North Staffordshire (later to become the University of Keele) or, in the sixties, of new universities such as Sussex or Kent. Similarly, the Council for National Academic Awards (CNAA – the body responsible for validating HE courses in non-university institutions) has also made possible innovations such as modular degree schemes, Diplomas of Higher Education and the novel courses by Independent Study developed by the North East London Polytechnic (now, the Polytechnic of East London) (Robbins 1988).

With the passage of time, curricular innovation has sometimes been undermined by structural pressures for conformity (for example, the re-emergence of quasi-single honours degrees within certain modular or combined degree schemes). It would be interesting to ponder how far such a regression to the conventional has been strengthened by the absence of new conceptions of quality deliberately designed to match these innovatory courses: conceptions, that is, framed in terms distinct from the traditional model in which quality tends to be regarded as largely an attribute of disciplinary knowledge.

When analysed, most degree courses in England and Wales seem to be structured around one of two organizing principals – the academic discipline or the profession. (Because Scottish HE is distinctive in several respects I shall exclude it from my comments.)

Degrees organized around a discipline, or cluster of related disciplines, are typically defined in terms of subject content, an accepted corpus of knowledge. Usually, very little attempt is made to specify their outcomes in terms accessible to a non-subject specialist. Their standard of quality is commonly regarded as comparability with similar degrees elsewhere, or is measured by the extent to which a degree course provides an adequate preparation for research in the discipline. (It is generally assumed, for instance, that a student graduating with first, or upper-second class honours, will be capable of proceeding directly to research in the disciplinary field concerned.)

In discipline-based courses the main forces for curricular change will tend to be those springing from the advancement of knowledge and shifts in focus within the discipline, or from the progress of staff research. Thus, for example, papers on women's history, ethnic history or a study of the debate over the reasons for British economic decline may come to be added to a degree course in History (Boys *et al* 1988, pp. 21–38). But there may be other forces at work, too, such as a desire to prepare graduates for employment, or to cope with straitened resources. A totally new course in computer familiarization may be added to the History degree, or efforts may be made to re-present and give greater emphasis to long-standing elements – such, for example, as the preparation of a dissertation – which are thought to be of value to later employment. Although changes in the environment outside the higher educational institution may stimulate some change and innovation within its disciplinary courses, it is likely to be piecemeal, to concern content rather than pedagogy, and generally to expand the syllabus, rather than to restructure it. These changes are unlikely, too, to lead to a redefinition of the nature of quality.

The clearest examples of degree courses organized around a profession are in fields such as Medicine or Engineering where the course is recognized only if it is accredited by the appropriate professional body as satisfying its – sometimes very detailed – requirements. However, even in relatively new vocational fields such as Business Studies or Hotel and Catering Management, where the power of a professional body is less preponderant, the content of a course is still likely to be tailored to the perceived needs of the vocation.

The most powerful source of curricular change in these courses will be alterations in the requirements of the professional body which, though often involving additional content, may also lead to the specification of particular forms of teaching or assessment. Here, too, it appears probable that there will be stronger pressure for the addition of subject matter than for its removal. Although, one might expect definitions of quality in such courses to be more responsible to changes in the external environment than in those structured around a discipline it is not obvious that this is always the case. Some professional bodies have displayed great attachment to the most traditional academic measures of excellence (eg, the A-levels of students on entry to a course) as means by which to uphold the status of their profession.

Both these models of curricular organization have considerable merits and have proved themselves over many years. Both, for example, furnish the student with a clear source of definition and reference point for study.

But, as Basil Bernstein has argued (Bernstein 1971), the discipline-based course by having, what he describes as, a high degree of 'framing', gives the student and teacher less control over '...the selection, organization and pacing of the knowledge transmitted in the pedagogical relationship' (Ibid., p.50). In consequence, it exposes them less to problems of choice and identity, and protects them against insecurity – and even, possibly, provides some insurance against poor teaching. (It may be the case, for example, that students can survive by means of dependence on textbooks on a badly taught conventional disciplinary course, in a way that would be quite impossible for those on a badly run cross-disciplinary learner-centred course.)

What is more, the discipline has undoubtedly proved a powerful engine for the advancement of knowledge in the past (although it now appears that an increasing proportion of research probably takes place in research communities organized at either the sub-disciplinary, or the cross-disciplinary level). The tradition of the disciplinary community gives a tested framework of intellectual coherence.

Similarly, the profession has served as an important channel of communication between the academy and a wider social constituency. Among other things is has provided a means by which practitioners, employers and the government could help to shape the content and processes of higher educational qualifications.

Nonetheless, both principles of organization also have their weaknesses. A course structured around the requirements of the practice of a discipline will not necessarily be the best way of meeting the needs of the vast majority of students who will cease to practice that discipline on graduation.

Indeed, the conventional disciplinary framework – which continues to be the main principle of organization in British higher educational institutions – provides an environment within which it is hard to examine the most fundamental problems of higher education – Who should learn what? And how? That is because its very existence begs the central question to be examined: whether the academic discipline, in fact, provides the most appropriate principle of organization for higher education courses in the future.

Similarly, a course structured around the requirements of a professional body may not necessarily be the best preparation for the many students who, while continuing in their general professional field, move into areas of it – such as management – where their expertise is not directly utilized. Still less is it likely to be appropriate for those who enter other fields, or for – what many predict will be – the increasing numbers of people who, in the future, will make one, or more, radical changes of occupation during their careers.

Indeed, the speed of social and technological change may prove to be so rapid that a course organized around the present, and predicted, needs of a profession may turn out even to be a poor preparation for the needs of that profession itself a decade later.

Neither model tends to encourage responsiveness to wider social forces nor to promote educational accountability. Neither leads to the definition of explicit learning outcomes, nor establishes public criteria of performance which would enable non-academics or non-professionals to reach an informed understanding of the standard of a course. In both cases, judgements about quality are made behind a veil of inexplicit aims and arcane criteria which are accessible only to restricted groups of professional educationalists – largely the very groups involved in providing such courses.

The emergence of new stakeholders in British higher education

For many years, it has been acknowledged that higher education in a developed, democratic country is necessarily an enterprise which legitimately touches, and involves, many different groups. Only recently, however, has the insight underlying this recognition been taken further: to the point where such groups have come to be regarded as 'stakeholders' in higher education. These stakeholders are usually taken to include – among others – academics, students (and their parents), professional bodies, employers, and representatives of the wider society (whom some might identify simply as the government). Although all will have certain common interests, each will also have special interests, some of which may conflict with those of other stakeholders.

This is not the place to discuss in detail how and why – and how completely – such shifts have taken place in public perceptions of higher education, but it is worth observing, however, that they seem to have accompanied a general questioning of established orthodoxies, a growing questioning of the claims of professional groups to omniscient wisdom, and a general decline in deference. They have also taken place over a period when the interdependence of higher education and industry has been becoming much more obvious, and during which a (modest) expansion has been taking place in entry to higher education.

What is noticeable about the models of curricular organization discussed above (the discipline based and the professionally-based) is that neither gives much weight to the needs of two of the major stakeholders: the students or the wider society.

The participation of employers in higher education is less clear. Certainly, they do exert a substantial influence over the curriculum of many professional degrees and, to a lesser extent, of some disciplinary degrees. However, it is not obvious that this has served as a means to press their general, non-vocationally specific requirements: their need, for example, for what the Council for Industry and Higher Education has come to term 'skilled brainpower' (CIHE 1987, 1). That is, for well-rounded and competent graduates displaying competence, adaptability and versatility.

It is even less clear what mechanisms exist to transmit to higher education the future needs of employers, especially those in rapidly changing sectors, including those that may be insignificant today, but could turn out to be of central importance in the economic world of the year 2020 (a time when today's entrants to HE will be reaching the peak of their careers).

Needs such as these, I contend, can be met only by strategic curricular development which stretches across the HE system (and into the schools and further education as well) – not by involvement of particular employers with particular degrees, valuable though that may be for other purposes.

In summary, both the models of course organization which I have discussed lead to change in the curriculum. Neither, however, in itself, constitutes an adequate mechanism for curricular development in higher education.

The aims of strategic curricular development in higher education

Curricular development in the full sense, shown by the examples I have drawn from 16–19 education, would, I suggest, entail five characteristics. First, at the most general level, it would have to be based on a strategic conception of the role of higher education in the circumstances of a particular society at a particular time. By 'strategic' I mean a perspective that goes beyond the particular circumstances in which higher educational institutions find themselves and tries to elucidate the various ways in which they may realise what they take to be their long-term missions (which may, of course, vary greatly from one institution to another).

Second, it would need to take account of the views and interests of all relevant stakeholders, not simply the educational producers.

Third, it would require the clientele of HE to be defined and recognition given to the various – possible conflicting – perceptions of their needs.

Fourth, it would involve translating these into specified outcomes and determining criteria for evaluating how far these were met. (Establishing, that is, new conceptions of quality.)

Finally, it would require that choices were made as to what forms of curriculum, pedagogy and assessment would be the most effective for realizing the specified outcomes with the particular student clientele and a given level of resources. Naturally, the whole process would require that a series of decisions be made on the best balance between conflicting ends.

Curricular development in this thorough-going sense certainly does not yet exist in British higher education. Nonetheless, certain institutions seem to be moving towards it; some, in collaboration with one of the few national initiatives which encourages widespread curricular development in higher education: the Enterprise in Higher Education initiative (EHE).

The Enterprise in Higher Education initiative

EHE is a programme which was launched by the, then, Manpower Services Commission (MSC – now, the Training Agency [TA]) in December 1987, with the support of the Department of Education and

Science and its Scottish and Welsh counterparts. (Glover 1990; Jones 1988; Macnair 1990).

The initiative took shape as a result of consultations, early in 1987, between the Secretary of State for Education and Science, the Secretary of State for Employment, the Chairs of the Higher Education funding bodies (the, then, National Advisory Body for Local Authority Higher Education [NAB] and the University Grants Committee [UGC]), heads of colleges, polytechnics and universities, employers and senior officials of the Manpower Services Commission.

The launch followed lengthy consultation with leading representatives of higher education and the HE funding bodies.

The purpose of EHE was, and is, to assist higher educational establishments, in partnership with employers, to bring about changes in their courses that will make them more responsive to the needs of employment and prepare their students more fully for their lives after graduation.

Higher educational institutions (HEIs) were invited to submit individual enterprise plans which show how, over a period of five years, they would make it possible for all their students to '...be able to develop competencies and aptitudes relevant to enterprise', which will be acquired '... at least in part, through project-based work, designed to be undertaken in a real economic setting, ... jointly assessed by employers and the higher educational institution' (MSC 1987).

The maximum funding normally available from the MSC/TA was £1 million over five years, which would be conditional upon the institution raising significant support from employers – in cash or kind. This would be at least the equivalent of 25 per cent of the MSC's funding over the first two years' and a 'substantial' proportion thereafter.

In addition, the proposals would have to fulfil five other requirements: be closely integrated into an institution's existing educational provision; to provide a plan for the staff development to support the changes proposed; to specify outcomes; to be monitored and evaluated by the institution itself; and, finally, to include a commitment that the programme would be sustained after MSC funding had come to an end.

In the first round, in 1988, 82 HE institutions submitted bids. (A further 83 bids were subsequently received under an ancillary scheme which made available a sum of £50,000 for one year to enable institutions to prepare themselves to apply for full funding.) In 1989, 63 bids were received for round two and, in 1990, a further 60 for rounds three and four. In all, around 135 colleges, polytechnics and universities have applied to one, or more, of the three invitations – well over half those entitled to do so. This has resulted in 11 being awarded full funding in 1988–9 and a further 15 in 1989–90, together with seven receiving development funding in 1988 – all of whom were later to receive full funding. (The results of rounds three and four are to be announced in the late summer of 1990.)

Distinctive features of EHE
Several features make EHE distinctive and, I would contend, justify it being regarded as one of the few examples of strategic curricular development in British higher education.

To begin with, it was deliberately designed not to be prescriptive. HEIs were encouraged, within the criteria listed above, to make a wide-ranging assessment of the position in which they found themselves in order to arrive at their own definitions of enterprise and to make their own decisions as to the best ways of realizing it. Interestingly, some found this a novel – even, on occasion, a disquieting – experience. This reaction supports my earlier observations on the lack of curricular development in HE and reinforces the view that the curriculum and pedagogy have generally been regarded either as naturally given, or as externally imposed: not as subjects on which an institution should exercise choice.

Another distinctive feature of EHE is partnership between employers and HEIs. Naturally there is nothing new in contacts with employers. Most establishments of any size have a long record of co-operation spanning a variety of fields such as research, consultancy, the provision of short courses, teaching companies and, in some cases, arrangements for student work placement.

Nonetheless, such links have hitherto typically involved movements back and forward across a boundary rather than the collaborative exploitation of a shared terrain. Seldom, for instance, have employers been encouraged to take part in the design and assessment of courses; seldom, too, have academics ensured that work placement – where it exists – has been fully integrated into the aims, learning experience and assessment of their courses. Rarely too, have employers played a part in defining the standards of a course or in measuring the performance of students against them.

In contrast, the aim, within EHE, of partnerships with employers is precisely to bring into being shared activity and to take advantage of the world of work as a means of enriching the experience of students. In seeking to involve employers in the definition of the aims and criteria of higher education – as well, of course, as the students themselves – EHE begins to make it possible for these previously inconspicuous stakeholders to develop their own conceptions of HE alongside those of the producers.

In another way, too, EHE contributes to the growth of a more open and externally accessible debate about the proper aims, nature of higher education, and the concepts of quality appropriate to them. It does this by its emphasis on objectives and outcomes. Each EHE proposal is a plan for the attainment of the institution's own explicit aims by means which it has – itself – deliberately chosen. If the proposal is selected, these are then translated into a contract between the HEI and the training agency which will embody, on a year-by-year basis, the institution's chosen aims, and the specific targets by which it has decided to monitor their achievement. The preparation and execution of such plans and contracts naturally tends to render the implicit explicit and to make the natural and the apparently given seem problematic. In doing so it concentrates attention on the need for deliberate decisions to be made. It also makes possible greater insight into the taken-for-granted assumptions of the academic world and opens to conscious examination the efficacy of traditional patterns of teaching and course organization. What is more, it begins to open to public scrutiny and establish as a topic of legitimate debate a whole cluster of questions related to the quality of the outcomes of higher education. In doing so, it makes possible an evaluation of the most effective ways of attaining these.

Such processes seem likely to establish chains of accountability in higher education where previously these were absent or tenuous: they encourage an HEI to be precise about how, and to what extent, it is accountable to its students, employers or society generally. They also promote accountability within the institution by linking the provision of resources for groups of staff in teaching departments to the achievement of overt, pre-defined elements of curricular change.

Finally, EHE is novel in that it aims explicitly to assist institutions in bringing about structural and cultural changes which will be both thorough-going and permanent. It does this by requiring that enterprise programmes should be closely integrated into the fabric of courses – not 'bolt-on' – and should be sustained after the cessation of TA funding. This is of central importance – as is demonstrated by the experience of many previous attempts at innovation. Forces for change tend to atrophy or be diverted unless effective mechanisms have been prepared to consolidate and sustain them when the initial stimulus is removed.

The issues that have emerged out of EHE

The first round of EHE programmes began to run in October 1988, the second round a year later. Since then the scheme has thrown up several new issues, and cast into high relief some which, before, seemed relatively insignificant. I shall refer to five.

The first, and perhaps the most important, has been the problem of how the quality of the student's experience is to be measured. This becomes an issue precisely because EHE encourages institutions to make explicit what they are trying to achieve, and to assess how successful they are in doing so. Hitherto, the performance indicators in use in Britain generally set out only to measure inputs. (For example, student-staff ratios or cost full-time-equivalent student.) On the rare occasions when they sought to measure outputs (eg, relative degree classifications) the meaning and validity of the units of measurement concerned have been – to put it kindly – obscure. (Cave *et al* 1988) Even the mechanisms for quality control derived from the CNAA – though fuller – have been of little help. They generate almost no information on what is actually achieved on a course and dwell rather, as Adelman and Alexander have pointed out (1982, p. 17), on the intentions of staff – not the outcomes for students.

The second has been the problem of how to link curricular development into the priorities of managers of HE institutions. Although many see EHE as a key component of their strategic planning, they nonetheless have to work in a world where they must cope with numerous other pressures – some of which appear to pull in directions opposed to the aims of EHE.

What is more, some would argue that there are few, if any, means by which institutions are rewarded for effectiveness in fulfilling their missions, especially if these give priority to the quality of students' learning. It could be said that the main factors affecting the status and prosperity of English higher educational institutions have been their closeness, historically, to sources of legitimacy and high status – not their effectiveness (about which very little has been known). If British HEIs are to change to meet new requirements it is obvious that there will have to be means that reward those that do so.

The third issue prompted by EHE is that of how to raise the prominence of staff development aimed at raising the quality of the students' learning. Many factors, not least the weight of traditional academic culture and established procedures for promotion and resource allocation, give primacy to research and publication and make the facilitation of learning appear unproblematic – if not unimportant. Again, greater emphasis on the quality of the learning that higher education provides for its students seems to depend upon substantial changes in the system by which status and rewards are distributed within universities, polytechnics and colleges.

Fourth, there is the problem of how best to capture the enthusiasm of employers and to reassure them that they have much to contribute to fields such as the design and assessment of courses which have previously been regarded in most cases as the preserve of academics. A great deal of attention, it seems, needs to be devoted to collaborative staff development between higher education and employment, that might begin to bridge the social and cultural divide between them. This is not easy: as Corelli Barnett and others have observed (Barnett 1986; Weiner 1981; Wright 1989) the divide, in Britain, between industry and higher education is both deep, of long standing and, to some extent, reinforced by the expectations that each has of the other.

The final issue is student participation. The obverse of over-directive teaching has often been passivity and deference among students. There can be no doubt that active learning in which the student takes greater responsibility, and which gives prominence to personal competence, is potentially threatening to students – and for that matter to staff also. Advances seem possible only to the extent that there are changes in the expectations that potential students have of higher education. These may now be taking place under the impact of changes, already mentioned, in the education of those aged 14–19.

Conclusion

EHE has been one of the very few examples of curricular development in British higher education. As a result, it has led to one of the few self-conscious attempts to redefine the purpose of higher educational courses in terms other than those simply of disciplinary knowledge, or the requirements of a professional body. By its emphasis on explicit outcomes, accountability, and the involvement of new partners it has thrown revealing light on the central issues that British higher education will have to address if it is re-interpret its mission to meet the challenges of its rapidly changing environment. It has begun to stimulate new definitions of quality and of the criteria for evaluating them.

Notes

1. An earlier version of this paper was presented to the 11th Annual Forum of the European Association for Institutional Research (EAIR) at the University of Trier, BRD, August 1989.

2. In April 1989 the government decided to raise the level of student fees on undergraduate courses from £607 to £1,675 p.a from the beginning of the academic years 1990–91. Although the grants made by the two funding bodies (the Polytechnics and Colleges Funding Council [PCFC] and the Universities Funding Council [UFC]) have been reduced to compensate. This has, nonetheless, acted as a stimulant for expansion – some institutions having recruited students for whom no grant had been made and who were, thus, funded solely by fee-income. (In the UK the fees of home students are almost invariably paid by their Local Education Authorities.)

3. In my discussion I shall concentrate on higher education in England and Wales because the system in Scotland is significantly different. Among the more striking distinctions are: that post–16 academic education is less specialized and has more connection with post–16 vocational education than in England and Wales; that the proportion of young people entering HE is higher (21.5 per cent in 1988/9); and that most higher educational institutions draw their students primarily from their local region.

   The Enterprise in Higher Education initiative, however, covers Scotland as well as England and Wales, but not Northern Ireland.

4. The drop in the numbers of young people is most unlikely to be paralleled by the same proportional fall in entrants to higher education because the decrease is least among the professional and managerial classes who supply some two-thirds of all entrants to higher education but, in fact, constitute less than a third of the total population (Smithers and Robinson 1989; Pearson *et al* 1989). Nonetheless, if other factors remain constant, it still seems probable that the total numbers of 18-year old entrants to higher education will decline significantly towards the mid–1990s. This fall could become much more marked if, as seems possible, employers increase their direct recruitment from the same, small pool of qualified young people as higher education.

5. A further major example of curriculum change in 16–19 education has become apparent since this article was originally drafted. It is

the work of the Schools Examinations and Assessment Council (SEAC), at the invitation of the Secretary of State for Education and Science, to consider how 'core skills' should be promoted through A-level and AS-level courses (SEAC 1990).

Note This paper expresses only the personal views of the author. It should not be read as a statement of the policy of the Training Agency.

References

Adelman, C. and Alexander, R. J. (1982) *The Self-Evaluating Institution: practice and principles in the management of educational change*. London: Methuen.

Boys, C et al (1988) *Higher Education and the Preparation for Work*. London: Jessica Kingsley.

Barnett, C. (1986) *The Audit of War: the illusion and reality of Britain as a great nation*. London: Macmillan.

Bernstein, B. (1971) On the classification and framing of educational knowledge. *In* M. F. D. Young (ed.) *Knowledge and Control: New directions in the sociology of education*. London: Collier-Macmillan.

Cave, M., Hanney, S. and Kogan, M. (1988) *Performance Indicators in Higher Education: a critical analysis of developing practice*. London: Jessica Kingsley.

Council for Industry and Higher Education (CIHE) (1987) *Towards a Partnership*. London: CIHE.

DES (Department of Education and Science) (1987) *Higher Education: meeting the challenge*. London: HMSO.

DES (1988): *Statistical Bulletin 6/88: Statistics of Schools in England*. London: DES.

Glover, D. (1990) *Enterprise in Higher Education: a briefing for employers*. Cambridge: CRAC.

Jones, A. (1988) The Manpower Services Commission's Enterprise in Higher Education initiative. *Industry and Higher Education* 2 (2), pp.117–119.

Macnair, G. (1990) The British Enterprise in Higher Education Initiative. *Higher Education Management* 2 (1), pp.60–71.

MSC (Manpower Services Commission) (1987) *Enterprise in Higher Education: guidelines for applicants*. Sheffield: MSC.

Pearson, R., Pike, G., Gordon, A. and Weyman, C. (1989) *How Many Graduates in the 21st Century ?, the Choice is Yours*: IMS Report No 177. Brighton, Sussex: Council for Industry and Higher Education/Institute of Manpower Studies.

Robbins, D. (1988) *The Rise of Independent Study: the politics and the philosophy of an educational innovation, 1970–1987*. Milton Keynes: Open University Press.

Royal Society of Arts (1990) *More Means Different*. London, RSA.

SEAC (Schools Examination and Assessment Council) (1990) *Examinations Post-16: Developments for the 1990s*. London: SEAC.

Smithers, A. and Robinson, P. (1989) *Increasing Participation in Higher Education*. London: British Petroleum Educational Services.

Weiner, M. (1981) *English Culture and the Decline of the Industrial Spirit, 1850–1980*. Cambridge: Cambridge University Press.

Wright, P. W. G. (1988): Rethinking the Aims of Higher Education. *In* H. Eggins (ed.) *Restructuring Higher Education: the Proceedings of the Annual conference of the Society for Research into Higher Education, 1987*. Milton Keynes: Open University Press.

Wright, P. W. G. (1989) Access or Exclusion ? Some comments on the history and future prospects of continuing education in England, London. *Studies in Higher Education*, Vol. 14, No. 1, pp. 23–40.

Chapter Seven
Quality and Resource Allocation
Gareth Williams

Quality in higher education is largely intangible and unquantifiable: resources are all too tangible and quantifiable. Nevertheless, there is an obvious link between resources and quality. In principle, at least, the higher the unit of resource the greater are the possibilities for improving quality. Conversely if there is severe competition between institutions for resources it is important to ensure that quality is not sacrificed in order to meet more readily identifiable quantitative indicators of performance.

The link is by no means automatic. Extra resources may be wasted and in any market competition between suppliers can be about quality as well as about price. Quality is by no means simply dependent on resources. Questions of quality arise in any consideration of such matters as professional integrity, fiduciary responsibilities of academic staff to their students and the intrinsic worth of academic excellence. Conversely, funding of higher education institutions does not necessarily have to take quality considerations into account. It can be argued that until recent years systematic quality judgements were not made by the UGC in its funding of universities. It can equally be argued, however, that the UGC's relationships with universities were such that it was able to take a uniform high standard of British universities for granted.

Quality assurance mechanisms
It was certainly the case that, until the 1980s, questions of quality in the university sector were very largely a matter for independent chartered institutions and in practice, although university senates had ultimate formal responsibility, effective quality control was usually maintained at the departmental level.

The only significant exception was qualifications which gave the right to professional practice or particular privileges with respect to professional examinations. In these cases professional institutes and associations accredited university courses, although their concern was primarily with course content rather than other indicators of quality. In the non-university institutions quality assurance has always been determined by outside agencies. However, a clear distinction was maintained between the quality assurance functions of the CNAA and the funding of these institutions through the Advanced Further Education Pool and the DES.

Both these models of quality assurance, the academic self-regulation of the universities and the external academic validation by the CNAA depended ultimately on a view of higher education which was essentially producer controlled. This was by no means unique to higher education. Many areas of economic activity which depended on professionals with high levels of specialist expertise were regulated in the same way. At one level it is inevitable that this must be so. Who can really judge whether a brain surgeon or an astronomer is doing a good job except another brain surgeon or astronomer?

Quality and competition

This model is disturbed when institutions are in direct competition with each other. A monopolistic market need present few problems. A monopoly supplier has a interest in maintaining high standards of service and is able to set prices at a level which makes this possible. It is usual for monopolistic competition between suppliers to take the form of quality competition rather than price competition. Where, as in British higher education until the 1980s, a uniform price was in effect set by a single monopolistic buyer and competition between institutions for their student clients was inevitably very largely based on quality. The advertising prospectuses of universities and polytechnics emphasized the comparative advantages of particular institutions with respect to such matters as academic reputation, availability of accommodation, pastoral care, pleasantness of surroundings and for postgraduate students research reputation. This did not work perfectly and few people who were at universities in the quarter century following the end of the war would agree that the practice always lived up to the promise but most accepted that quality was helped by favourable staff-student ratios and well equipped laboratories and libraries.

Reputation was important and informal pressures within higher education institutions were usually sufficient to deal with cases where reputation was seriously threatened by lapses of quality. Apart from very rare cases of serious dereliction of professional responsibilities which could be dealt with by disciplinary action, there was in general sufficient slack in the system to enable incompetent lecturers and ineffective researchers to be bypassed or eased into other responsibilities.

Mass and elite systems of higher education

It was not necessarily an ideal system but it was one that worked as an elite system of higher education. The essence of an elite is that those who are chosen accept that they must maintain certain standards and the worst penalty they can suffer is to lose their elite status.

Nearly all these assumptions become invalid when an elite system of higher education becomes a mass system, and the assumptions of professional self-regulation become inoperable when monopolistic pricing gives way to market competition.

This is the situation in which British higher education finds itself as it enters the 1990s. It is being transformed into a mass higher education system and it is being funded as a competitive higher education system.

It has been recognized ever since Martin Trow invented the idea in the 1960s that mass higher education means great diversity. There must be a broad spectrum of students with many different aims, interests, approaches to learning, previous educational achievement and modes of study. Their teachers will be correspondingly diverse. Some will be leading researchers, others will be professional practitioners, others with practical experience in industry or commerce and some will have particular abilities to help students whose previous experience of education has been unproductive. Some will be excellent at delivering mass lectures, others at small group teaching and still others at facilitating student-centred learning. The assurance of quality in such a system is more difficult than in the relatively homogenous elite system. It is also more important.

Problems of quality assurance

The assurance of quality in the current situation of British higher education is difficult because quality must be related to what Christopher Ball has called 'fitness for purpose'. Different criteria, different standards and different methods of appraisal are appropriate for both students and teachers undertaking different kinds of courses or performing different functions. One of the criticisms that has been widely made of British higher education during the past decade or so is that it has attempted to develop mass participation on the assumptions of an elite system. The single-subject honours degree was at the centre of this system. Most students, staff and institutions have been forced into this particular mould and most courses have been assessed in relation to criteria that are appropriate for this kind of high level academic qualification.

Appraisal has not until now been a systematic feature of career development of academic staff. However, informal appraisals and evaluations of staff performance for promotion or for job selection have until the late 1980s depended very heavily upon the assumptions of the elite academic model. Publications, research record and, where it has been taken into account at all, the ability to convey information to large groups of students, have been the main criteria. Financial pressures from the mid-1980s onwards have brought about some modification and ability to raise money and the ability to develop and maintain good contacts with certain external agencies have begun to appear as criteria in the appointment of senior staff in universities, polytechnics and colleges.

Institutions have been similarly judged largely according to a single linear scale of academic value. Those with the most highly regarded honours degrees have tended to be at the top of any ranking and those with relatively low proportions of students doing degree course have been at the bottom. Such rankings have created self-fulfilling prophecies in that highly rated institutions attract the best students and this has added to their prestige. Paradoxically it is possible that the absence of any formal ranking of institutions may have helped to create this single scale of values. In the absence of any formal ranking, institutions at the bottom of the list have found it more worthwhile to try to imitate institutions at the top rather than to recognize that they have no chance of competing with them on those particular criteria and to develop instead their own distinctive approaches. However, it would be misleading to pretend that there have not been substantial changes in recent years and institutional diversity is now much more widely accepted by staff, students and educational planners.

Access

Effective systems of quality assurance are important in a mass system of higher education because diversity can be very misleading to students. This is extremely important in considering questions of access. Access to higher education for its own sake is a dubious privilege. It can be argued that undergoing a course of higher education is worthwhile only if students receive some tangible benefit from it. If students are cajoled into higher education with an expectation that they will receive all the benefits of a good honours degree from a highly regarded university and in fact are offered third rate educational experiences which result in their dropping out after the first year, the most charitable comment is that they have been misled.

It has often been said, but it is worth repeating, that when access to higher education was confined to highly motivated young people coming to university directly from an intensive secondary education it was reasonable to assume that within broad limits they could take care of themselves. Now that higher education is being opened up to school leavers who are not sure of their own motivation and who have not performed particularly well in secondary education, and to adults who have not studied seriously for several years, then there is a far greater responsibility on providers to ensure that the educational experience is worth having, and suited to the needs and interests of the students.

Quality and funding mechanisms

All these are intrinsic issues of quality which arise as a result of the transition from elite to mass higher education. They are compounded when the transition is accompanied by a shift away from institutional funding on a grant maintained basis towards payment for specific services rendered. Since quantity is much easier for outside observers to identify and measure than quality it is inevitable that payment by results should take more account of quantitative than qualitative indicators. If institutions were funded simply on an average price per student basis with no concern for the outputs it would be inevitable that institutions would have an interest in concentrating expansion in courses that were cheap to provide. If income is received through student fees it is essential to ensure that any implicit contract with student customers is based upon a realistic statement of what the institution is offering each individual student. This is partly a moral issue. It should be considered unethical to mislead students about what they have a right to expect in return for their fee payments. It is also an issue of long-term marketing strategy as markets both depend on and generate information. Institutions which fail to live up to their promises risk losing the most saleable asset of any higher education institution, its reputation.

Guaranteed quality may well become a matter of litigation. So far it has not been common practice in Britain for students to sue their teachers though there has been a steady trickle of cases in recent years. However, as the market ethos becomes more prevalent it is not at all unlikely that litigation will become more common if students believe they have been misled. It is possible to imagine that judges and juries would take a severe view of institutions which had misled young people into wasting several years of their lives, and not inconsiderable amounts of money, with misleading promises about the services that were being offered. There is in principle little difference between the implied contract in a package holiday brochure and that of a university or polytechnic prospectus.

So far the discussion has been couched in general terms and has attempted to identify intrinsic issues that arise in the transition from elite to mass higher education and from a deficiency grant funded to a market financed system. The most important specific feature of higher education funding in Britain in the 1990s is that about half the income of universities and two-thirds of that of non-university institutions comes from the respective funding bodies, the UFC and the PCFC. Both have instituted sets of arrangements whereby universities, polytechnics and colleges bid for funds on a unit cost basis.

There are, of course, differences of detail as the systems have developed so far. The PCFC has invited bids for incremental students at prices to be determined by polytechnics and colleges, while the UFC invites bids for all students at what are, in effect, standard prices. At the same time government is taking steps to ensure that student fees are high enough to cover the marginal cost of student places in any institution which still has any spare physical capacity. All higher education institutions will be under considerable pressure to increase student numbers and to reduce average costs. It is, indeed, an explicitly stated government policy to increase student numbers during the 1990s much more than increases in public funding. The pressure on institutions to introduce what may well come to be called flexible quality criteria as an aspect of the inevitable diversity of mass higher education will become considerable.

It has been widely reported that when faced with a similar situation with respect to overseas students in the early 1980s in a period of severe financial stringency, not all universities were able to resist the temptation to compromise on quality as part of their marketing strategies. There will be great temptations to do the same for all students during the 1990s, and it will be relatively easy to disguise quality compromises as increases in flexibility, accessibility or variety.

The role of the funding agencies

There are two aspects of quality that need to be taken into account by funding agencies. One is to ensure that there are basic quality thresholds for each separate activity below which it would be inappropriate to provide public funds. The second is to establish criteria and mechanisms for encouraging innovation and above normal or 'premium' quality activities. In principle this distinction applies both to teaching and to research. Basic quality thresholds are best assured at the level of institutions with an external agency to ensure that viable quality assurance mechanisms are in place. All higher education institutions are now expected to offer a diverse range of courses, which evolve in response to changing consumer demands. No two institutions are precisely the same. External quality control mechanisms are almost certain to restrict the range of learning opportunities that are made available and in particular are unlikely to enable universities, polytechnics and colleges to respond quickly to new opportunities as and when they appear. External control is almost inevitably both excessively rigid and easily evaded and this is likely to result in providers of courses becoming alienated from the quality controllers. Quality assurance procedures that are externally imposed are more likely to be seen as regulations to be reluctantly complied with and evaded where possible. Quality is better assured if those who deliver higher education services have a sense of direct ownership of the quality assurance procedures both individually and institutionally. A course team which takes its own decisions to improve a course which is receiving adversely critical feedback from students is likely to respond more quickly than one which receives the same criticisms from an external funding or accreditation agency. It is important, however, for external agencies to ensure that suitable mechanisms are in place which will enable institutions to identify quality weaknesses and to act upon them quickly.

This is the idea behind both the current stance of the CNAA with respect to major PCFC institutions and the new Academic Audit Unit of the Committee of Vice Chancellors and Principals. Both are intended to ensure that universities, polytechnics and major colleges have appropriate quality assurance mechanisms in place.

Evidence of quality assurance mechanisms at the institutional level which need to be looked for include for example: explicit statements of ways in which quality will be monitored and assured within courses; suitable procedures for discovering and interpreting the responses of students to courses and mechanisms for feeding the information back into subsequent course development programmes; effective use of process indicators to demonstrate that the institution can diagnose and treat problems as they arise; evidence of a willingness to listen to and act upon information coming from employers of the institution's graduates; suitable criteria and procedures rigorously followed for the introduction of new courses; regular review procedures for existing courses to ensure that criteria that were met when the course was established continue to be met and that there are appropriate procedures for authorizing modifications in courses; procedures for the selection of external examiners to ensure that they are likely to be properly objective; explicit procedures which ensure that external examiners are able to exercise functions of independent peer review as well as moderation of examination marks and mechanisms to ensure that reports and recommendations from external examiners are fed into the formal decision making machinery of the institution. All these are quality assurance mechanisms which any well-run higher education institution ought to have in place. The job of an external agency is to ensure that this is the case and perhaps to make occasional spot checks to ensure that what is formally claimed for the procedures actually operates in practice.

Encouragement of premium quality is, however, inevitably in part a more direct concern of funding agencies. If they offer all institutions a standard price per student or undertake to fund only the lowest price institutional bids there will be no incentive for institutions to develop above average quality courses if this means above average costs. The funding agencies need to develop realistic mechanisms for operating dual criteria in allocating funds for teaching, similar to the way in which UFC uses multiple criteria for funding research. The PCFC has indeed begun to initiate a system in which courses are allocated to five bands according to HMI assessments of quality. Five bands seems excessive and it is significant that in the first year of operation only the top and bottom bands were used for resource allocation purposes, the top band being eligible for additional funding and the bottom band being considered disqualified from funds.

Funding of 'premium' quality
In considering the case for special funding for 'premium' quality it is essential to be clear about the reasons why some institutions should receive more money than others for doing apparently the same thing. Unless the criteria are explicit all institutions will provide evidence to show why they are a special case. There are, three such reasons.

1. Any system of formula funding depends upon dividing a very large number of discrete activities into a much smaller number of categories, nine programme areas in the case of the PCFC and twenty-two subject areas in the case of the UFC. It is inevitable that not all courses within each category are homogeneous. Some anomalies will occur and it is probable both that the funding agency will pitch its normal allocations towards the lower end of the range of resource costs within the category in order to encourage expansion at minimum cost. It is very important, therefore, to have the flexibility to provide adequate funds for desirable programmes that are intrinsically above the average costs for that category.

2. Most changes in students numbers are inevitably resourced, at least in part, on a marginal cost basis in that some of the 'up front costs' have already been covered by the established number of students. Thus established courses can adapt to gentle long-run pressure for reductions in average cost. There is no reason why a course in which no changes at all are made from year to year should not be able to sustain annual average cost reductions for a considerable period. No new library materials nor equipment would be necessary, and buildings and plants might be used more intensively by simply offering the same course to several groups of students. At the other extreme a brand new course must be funded initially on an above average long-run cost basis. New equipment, books and materials must be bought, staff must prepare the teaching materials and so on. A second reason for special funding for premium quality courses, therefore, is to permit and encourage innovation.

3. The third reason why a quality 'premium' might be paid is because of the intrinsic benefits of quality and its effect as an example on the rest of the system. If it is known that university 'x' or polytechnic 'y' is being rewarded for having a particularly good course in, say, engineering design, engineering designers from other institutions are likely to take steps to inform themselves about the nature of this course in order that they too may be able to make claims for premium payments. This raises questions of what indicators might be used to assess premium quality.

Some examples might be:

• where a course can demonstrate that its graduates are particularly favoured by employers as compared with others in the same programme;

- where a course is particularly attractive to students as indicated by the applications/enrolments ratio or qualifications of entrants;
- where a course is particularly successful in converting less well qualified entrants into successful graduates;
- where a course depends particularly heavily on high quality research and scholarship within the institution;
- where peer judgement within a programme area indicates that a course is particularly valuable and has good reason to incur above average costs.

In making premium payments it will be essential for funding agencies to distinguish between these three categories of payment. Where the premium is because of a high cost sub-discipline within a programme area this would be essentially a permanent subsidiary programme area and as long as these courses continue to run they would need to be able to claim premium allocations. It would therefore be essential that the criterion be used as sparingly as possible. Otherwise formulae would become extremely complicated with the likelihood eventually of each course having its own level of resource cost and no possibility of the funding agency deciding what the average cost ought to be. Where the premium allocation is required for innovation the premium payment by definition would need to be available only during the start-up period of a course. The payment could take the form of a certain percentage increase over the period during which the first intake of students passed through the course. The third category, the high quality exemplar, is more difficult. One-off prizes are unlikely to attract much serious attention unless they are very large. The nature of annual prizes is that panels of judges usually try to employ slightly different criteria from year to year so annual prizes might provide an incentive for other institutions to do something different from the award winning one in order to increase their chances of gaining a prize the following year. This would, at least in part, defeat the purpose of encouraging imitation. On the other hand it would clearly be inappropriate for a quality premium of this type to be built permanently into the funding machinery of a particular institution. Something between these two extremes is clearly necessary.

Another consideration is that the number of quality awards should be small enough to allow courses to be properly publicized and to enable the specific characteristics of the courses to be disseminated around the higher education system and so on. As a general rule the use by funding councils of the concept of premium quality in teaching would need to be used very sparingly. Otherwise the formula funding would simply collapse into a myriad of special cases and, furthermore, any pretence of institutional autonomy which formula funding and contract funding permit would be lost.

It would not, however, be difficult for a funding council to decide to allocate, say, 10 per cent of its total recurrent grant allocations for 'premium payments' of which, say, half might be for intrinsically expensive courses, a quarter for innovations which would be funded on the basis of a certain percentage addition to what would otherwise be the unit of resource at which institutions were funded, and a quarter for exemplary courses.

Conclusion

In summary a viable system of quality assurance for the 1990s would be one in which institutions are themselves responsible for ensuring minimum quality thresholds. The institutions themselves would have a collective interest in monitoring the arrangements of individual institutions to ensure that long-term prospects for the sector as a whole were not being undermined by quality short cuts. Responsibility for stimulating and rewarding specific examples of high quality teaching would need to be with the funding councils.

Indeed in a period in which the funding councils become minority contributors to the funding of higher education institutions and market pressures will come from students with, in effect, standard value vouchers in their pockets, the funding councils will have a particular responsibility in areas, where for any reason high quality was unlikely to be recognized immediately by students.

It is possible to envisage funding of innovation and quality improvement and subsidy of worthwhile courses for which student demand is insufficient, as the main resource allocation functions of the funding councils before the end of the century. Indeed it is possible to go further and envisage the main function of universities and polytechnics as institutions as being the assurance of quality in courses and other activities in departments that are effectively financially autonomous operating units.

Bibliography

Adleman, C. and Alexander, R. (1982) *The Self-Evaluating Institution: practice and principles in the management of educational change*. London: Methuen.

Aleamoni, L.M. and Hexner, P.Z. (1980) A review of the research on student evaluation and a report on the effect of different sets of instructions on student course and instructor evaluation. *Instructional science*, 9, pp. 67–84. An extensive review of the research concerning the effect of different variables on student ratings is presented. A study is then reported comparing the effects of different sets of instructions on student evaluations of the course and instructor. The results indicated that the students who were informed that the results of their ratings would be used for administrative decisions rated the course and instructor more favourably on all aspects than students who were informed that the results of their ratings would only be used by the instructor.

Anderson, A.W. (1983) *Academic staff views on criteria of teaching/excellence*. Perth, University of Western Australia, Research Unit in University Education, Occasional Paper, 4, 1983.
At Western Australia University a careful enquiry was conducted to obtain staff opinion as to (a) criteria of teaching competence and excellence; (b) acceptable evidence that a suitable level had been reached; and (c) methods of obtaining acceptable evidence. Response rate was only 88/550 (16 per cent), and it is not known if the sample is representative. The answers suggested that the four most important criteria of teaching ability were ability to communicate effectively; ability to generate student interest; organization of/preparation for/classes; personal attributes – reliability, practicality, interest in and enthusiasm for one's subject. The six most acceptable kinds of evidence were student opinion; quality of course materials; demonstration of interest in students; willingness to innovate; willingness to be monitored by suitably qualified persons; and peer assessment. The four best methods of obtaining evidence were student questionnaires; examination of course materials; observation – either live or video; and peer group evaluation.

Andreson, L.W. and Powell, J.P. (1987) Competent teaching and its appraisal. *Assessment and evaluation in higher education*, 12/1, Spring, pp. 66–72.
As professionals, academics can reasonably be expected to be competent in both teaching and research. In order to judge the competence of an

83

individual as a teacher it is necessary to establish the range of knowledge, skills and attitudes that constitute competence. It is argued that this is composed of three major elements: preparation for teaching, the engagement in teaching, and professional development as a teacher. The constituents of each component are then listed. The paper concludes by suggesting sources of evidence and urging the need for more attention to be given to the documentation of achievements related to teaching.

Arubayi, E. (1986) Students evaluation of instructions in higher education: a review. *Assessment and evaluation in higher education* 11/1, pp.1–10.
Reviews research work on subject and looks at views of proponents and opponents on student rating. Variables influencing students' evaluation of instruction are identified. Recommendations and conclusions are based the on review.

Arubayi, E.A. (1987) Improvement of instruction and teacher effectiveness: are student ratings reliable and valid? *Higher education*, 16/3, pp.267–78.
This paper reviews the evidence of whether student ratings are reliable and valid enough to be used for the purpose of the improvement of instruction and teacher effectiveness. The literature tends to show a measure of consistency, stability and validity of student ratings. Several variables such as sex of rater and ratee, class size, mood of students, rank of instructors, grades students were expecting, time of the day courses are taught, to mention only a few, have been found to have a low to high positive relationship, with student ratings. It also appears that the use of student ratings leads to the improvements of instruction, provided the evaluation data are fed back to the instructor and that an expert or consultant provides assistance to the instructor.

Astin, A. (1982) Why not try some new ways of measuring quality. *Education Review* Vol.63, Spring, pp.10–15.

AVCC (Australian Vice Chancellors' Committee) (1981) *Academic staff development*. Canberra: AVCC.

Avi-Itzhak, T. (1982) Teaching effectiveness as measured by student ratings and instructor self-evaluation. (University of Haifa, Israel), *Higher Education*, 11(6), pp.629–634.
The study was designed to evaluate teaching effectiveness based on effective teacher behaviours. 2,500 students enrolled in 125 courses evaluated their instructors on a five item, four point Likert scale questionnaire. Their instructors used a similar questionnaire to evaluate their own teaching. The findings of the study indicate a lack of agreement between students and their instructors on abstract instruction's attributes, but that agreement exists for attributes of a concrete nature.

Ball, C.J.E. (1985) *Fitness for purpose*. Guildford: SRHE & NFER/Nelson.

Ball, C. (1988) Keynote Speech. In Eggins, H. (ed). *Restructuring Higher Education: Proceedings of Annual Conference*. pp.3–12. Milton Keynes, SRHE/Open University Press.

Ball, C. and Eggins (eds) (1989) *Higher Education into the 1990s: new dimensions*. Milton Keynes: SRHE and Open University Press.

Ball, R. and Halwachi, J. (1987) Performance indicators in higher education. *Higher education*, 16/4, pp.393–405.
Interest has been increasing in many countries in assessing performance of higher education institutions (and also departments within institutions). Two important reports in the UK have recently advocated the use of performance indicators for this purpose. This paper argues that such indicators cannot be used in a meaningful way without a clear view of institutional goods. Problems of deriving such goal systems discussed and a critical review of work sort in this field is presented. Methodological problems associated with developing and using effective and useful performance indicators are described and research undertaken in this field underlined. Finally, the authors describe conditions under which they believe performance indicators may be used to give valid insights into performance of institution or departments.

Banta, T., Fisher, H. and Minkel, C. (1986) Assessment of Institutional Effectiveness at the University of Tennessee, Knoxville. *International Journal of Institutional Management in Higher Education* Vol.10 No.3.

Barnett, C. (1986) *The Audit of War: the illusion and reality of Britain as a great nation*. London: Macmillan.

Barnett, R.A. (1987) The maintenance of quality in the public sector of the UK higher education. *Higher Education* 16/3, pp.279–301.
Since the establishment of the UK system of binary higher education in mid-1960s CNAA and the public sector institutions have evolved systems of quality maintenance. Key elements of interactions between CNAA and its associated institutions are identified. The shifting balance of responsibilities from the CNAA to the institutions is sketched. Some observations are made on course review in the public sector compared to university sector.

Becher, T. (1989) *Academic Tribes and Territories: intellectual enquiry and the culture of disciplines*. Milton Keynes: SRHE/Open University Press.

Becher, T. and Kogan, M. (1980) *Process and Structure in Higher Education*. London: Heinemann.

Bee, M. and Dolton, P. (1985) Degree Class and Pass Rates: an inter-university comparison. *Higher Education Review* Vol 7. No. 2, pp.45–52.

Bejar, I.I. (1975) A survey of selected administrative practices supporting student evaluations of instructional programs. *Research in higher education*

3, 1, pp.77–86.

A mail survey of 333 American universities was conducted to assess the current status of student evaluation of instruction. Based on a 68 per cent return, it was concluded that there has been an increase in the popularity of student ratings as a means of evaluating faculty performance, as well as an increase in the frequency with which evaluation results are used in decisions concerning faculty status. However, at most universities, research on the rating instruments does not seem to have kept pace with the decisions that are based on the rating instruments.

Bernstein, B. (1971) On the classification and framing of educational knowledge. *In* M.F.D. Young (ed) *Knowledge and Control: new directions in the sociology of education.* London: Collier-Macmillan.

Bogue, E.G. (1982) Allocation of public funds on instructional performance/ quality indicators. *International Journal of Institutional Management in Higher Education,* 6(1), pp.37–43.

In the United States, funding of public colleges and universities is almost entirely dependent on previous funding history and on the enrolment patterns of higher education institutions. If questions of performance are asked of colleges and universities, these are inevitably answered in terms of process, size and activity levels rather than outcomes and effectiveness. A performance funding policy implemented in the State of Tennesse links two per cent of state funding for higher education to achievement rather than activity, to outcomes rather than size. The policy has major implications for linking funding and performance in colleges, and in service-based institutions in both government and private sectors.

Booth B., and Booth, C. (1989) Planning for Quality: advice respectfully tendered to the PCFC. *Higher Education Quarterly* Vol.43, No.4, pp.278–288

Boud, D. (1988) Professional development and accountability: working with newly appointed staff to foster quality. *Studies in higher education* 13/2 pp.165–76.

Examines ways in which universities can assist new staff to develop their skills in 14 various aspects of their academic role and identifies the responsibilities of the universities and heads of department in this task. These issues are illustrated by reference to the case study of an Australian university that has recently accepted a department-based scheme for the professional development of academic staff. Noting the resistance that such a scheme can encounter, the author examines ways in which such schemes can be introduced sensitively.

Braksamp, L.A. (1984) *Evaluating teaching effectiveness: a practical guide.* Newbury Park, Ca.: Sage.

Brennan, J. (1986) Peer Review and Partnership: changing patterns of validation in the public sector of higher education in the United Kingdom.

International Journal of Institutional Management in Higher Education, Vol. 10 No. 2.
This paper describes the external system of course validation in the non-university sector of British higher education. It is a system under review as institutions seek greater autonomy and the state seeks greater control and more effective quality assurance. The implications of the changes in the system currently proposed are explored with reference to relationships within institutions and the balance of power between academic networks and institutional hierarchies.

Brew, A., and McCormick, B. (1979) Student learning and an independent study course. *Higher Education* 8 pp.429–441.

Brookfield, S. (ed) (1985) *Self-directed Learning: from theory to practice*. San Francisco: Jossey-Bass.

Brown, G. (1978) *Lecturing and explaining*. London: Methuen.

Browne, S. (1984) NAB and 'quality' in higher education. *Higher Education Review* Vol. 17 No. 1 pp.45–50.

Burdsal (C.A.) and Bardo, J.W. (1986) Learning students' perceptions of teaching: dimensions of evaluation. *Educational and Psychological Measurement* 46/1, pp.63–9.
Begins with a critical review of current approaches to the assessment of teaching. Multivariate procedures have improved the situation but several difficulties remain. A first and second order factor analysis study of 42,019 students' perceptions of teaching is described (between 1977 and 1982). A summary of factors is given. The first factor relates to Attitudes Towards Students, Work load, Course Value to Students, Course Organization Structure, Grading Quality and Level of Material. The second factors are general quality and general difficulty. The results challenge the idea of using single item indicators: those incorporated in the form were too simplistic; in any case a single score must be a poor measurement indicator. The contradicting findings between, eg students' perceptions and expected grades may be explained by the fact that many studies of assessment use non-factored summated scales which allow extraction of variables that cause difficulty. Student perceptions of teaching should be taken for what they are and, since there is a problem in defining 'good teaching', psychomatic measurements of their perceptions should be used. In this study quality was found to be unrelated to course difficulty and a multidimensional view of students' perceptions of teaching is supported.

Cannon, R.A. (1987) *The professional development of university teachers*. Institute for Higher Education, University of New England.
In this small book the author considers the problem of improving university teaching, with special regard to the nature of universities as organizations, to the characteristics and work of academic staff, and to the theory,

practice, and research on attempts to make teaching better. He concludes that prospects for beneficial change are not good but he does reprint and endorse a policy for staff development promulgated by the Australian Vice Chancellors' Committee. Though deliberately embedded in an Australian context, most of what is said has a much wider application.

Cave, M., Hanney, S. and Kogan, M. (1988) *Performance Indicators in Higher Education: a critical analysis of developing practice*. London: Jessica Kingsley.

Church, C.H. (1988) Qualities of validation. *Studies in higher education*, 13/1, pp.27–44.
Conventional wisdom in the public sector assures that there is a direct and tangible relationship between validation and both academic standards and the general quality of higher education provided in a given institution. This new way was to some measure accepted by government when it agreed to continue with CNNA rather than implement Lindop's (1985) recommendation that designated polytechnics should be given complete autonomy.

Quality and cost effectiveness are seen as coming largely from the proper application of techniques of validation. Pattern of course monitoring has long been current in polytechnics and other colleges. Validation is a necessary condition for quality control.

Inputs into higher education: admissions, staff and other resources and the curriculum. CVCP and NAB regard the quality of staff as the first safeguard of the quality of education in general (NAB 1984) report on quality. Must be present in adequate numbers, properly qualified and duly appointed. Also concerned that staff resources are fully exploited through personal induction programmes and then maintained at high level.

Cohen, P.A. (1980) Effectiveness of student rating feedback for improving college instruction: a meta-analysis of findings. *Research in higher education*, 13, pp.321–341.

Cohen, P.A. (1981) Student ratings of instruction and student achievement: a meta-analysis of multisection validity studies. *Review of educational research*, 51, pp.281–309.

Cole, C.C. (1982) *Improving instruction: issues and alternatives for higher education*. AAHE ERIC/Higher Education Research Report, 4.
Based on a review of more than 300 books and articles related to instructional improvement published since 1978, this monograph considers the importance of improving instruction from the perspective of faculty members, students, institutions, and society; discusses the implications of recent learning theories; examines issues and concepts related to instructional improvement; explores the relevance of faculty attitudes to the issue of instructional improvement; presents recent data on methods of instruction; and reviews recent research and suggests possibilities for future

research on improving instruction. The report concludes with eight major observations drawn from the literature review and a bibliography.

Council for Industry and Higher Education (CIHE) *Towards a Partnership*. London: CIHE.

Council for National Academic Awards (1986) Report to CAIP on the role of external examiners. *CNAA mimeograph*.

Council for National Academic Awards (1988) *Handbook*. London: CNAA.

Council for National Academic Awards (1989) Toward an educational audit. *Information Services Discussion Paper 3*. London: CNAA.

CNAA (1990[a]) *CNAA Annual Report for 1988-89*.

CNAA (1990[b]) *Changing Patterns of Course Review*.

Cowell, R. (1983) The changing contexts of appraisal: translating academic appraisal into institutional policy. *Studies in Higher Education*, 8(2), pp. 165–167.
The paper describes a level and method of appraisal which combines traditional academic and professional criteria with a range of comparative and contextual criteria drawn from the needs, demands, expectations and characteristics of an institution's markets. It is suggested that, as higher education enters a period of stringent questioning about its purposes and practices, this method of 'portfolio analysis' can generate answers and arguments which recognize and reconcile a variety of perspectives, notably those of students, academic staff, educational managers, employers, and local and central government. Such 'appraisal for justification' may well be the soundest and safest foundation for institutional policies at a time of centralized educational planning.

Craig, J.R. *et al* (1986) *Evaluating effective teaching in colleges and universities: how far have we come?* Annual meeting of the American Evaluative Association, Kansas City.

Croham Committee (1987) Review of the University Grants Committee. (Cmnd 81) London: HMSO.

Cross, K.P. (1987) *Feedback In The Classroom: making assessment matter*. Assessment Forum, American Association for Higher Education.

Cuthbert, R. (1988) Quality and Management in Higher Education. *Studies in Higher Education* Vol. 13 No.1, pp.59–68.
This paper examines the relationship between quality and management in higher education. It considers the nature of management, the meanings ascribed to management and related concepts such as leadership, and the appropriateness of these concepts in the context of higher education. These preliminary considerations provide a basis for considering the connections

that may exist between management performance and institutional performance. In addressing these issues, the paper aims to confront such questions as: what part does management play in ensuring high quality institutional performance? to what extent can judgements about management performance be separated from judgements about institutional performance? and so on. This necessitates consideration of how these kinds of performance can be judged, and the paper offers frameworks for analysing judgements of institutional and managerial performance.

CVCP (1986) *Performance indicators in universities: a first statement by a joint CVCP/UGC working group*. London: CVCP, July.

CVCP (1987) *Career development and staff appraisal procedures for academic and academic related staff (CVCP and AUT joint document)*. London: CVCP, November.

CVCP (1987c) *Appraisal, promotion procedures and probation: note to Vice Chancellors and Principals* (N87/108). London: CVCP, 2nd December.

De Neve, H.M.F. and Janssen, P.J. (1982) Validity of student evaluation of instruction. *Higher Education*, 11(5), pp.543–552.
A new type of questionnaire for the evaluation of instruction in higher education is described. The EVAluation of LECturing (Evalec) questionnaire is a content-valid evaluation instrument based on a teaching- learning model. It consists of 82 statements based on a theoretical description of 'good teaching' to which students respond according to a six point agreement scale. These 82 statements can be linked to seven lecture components. The instrument was given to a total of 765 first-year students. Factor analysis was used to explore the material for three separate groups of students. The results were reduced to scores on five perception scales which in turn could be reduced to three fundamental dimensions of behavioural aspects of study. A major advantage of the instrument is thus that individual items on the questionnaire may be located to a cell in a 7 × 5 matrix, each cell being defined by one of the seven components of 'good teaching' on which the Evalec is constructed, and by one of the five student perception dimensions. Consequently student perception can be transformed, in accordance with the teaching-learning model into particular educational advice for improving instruction. In this way the problem of giving relevant and feasible feedback to the lecturer is simplified.

DES (Department of Education and Science) (1987) *Higher Education: meeting the challenge*. London: HMSO

DES 4 (1989) *The English polytechnics: an HMI commentary*. London: HMSO.

De Winter Hebron, C. (1983) Performance evaluation of teaching: a diagnostic approach. *Higher Education in Europe*, 8(2), pp.5–17.

There are five ways of evaluating teachers and their teaching: (1) against a checklist of the key activities of teaching; (2) by concentrating on the course; (3) by measuring conformity to a set of predetermined ideological and/or formal criteria; (4) evaluation in terms of student performance; (5) by student evaluation of teachers and teaching. Behaviourally referenced student rating of teachers has a number of advantages: (1) the teacher is asked to specify his key objectives; (2) it records opinion on the teacher in questionnaire responses; (3) data can be compared with a 'nationally acquired data base'; (4) 'for each behaviour and objective, a closeness of connection is calculated for the data base' (5) 'where the teacher's mean performance scores are below those of the data base, and scores on objectives selected by the lecturer are too, the system points to those low performance scores most closely related to the low objective scores.' From his work, de Winter Hebron draws four conclusions: (1) simplistic models of teaching evaluation are inappropriate; (2) the most important single variable encountered by the student is probably the culture of the individual department or subject; (3) probably the most important models of student learning are the cognitive-psychology and information-processing ones; (4) transfer of findings about student learning or educational innovations needs careful handling.

De Winter Hebron, C. (1984) An AID for evaluating teaching in higher education. *Assessment and Evaluation in Higher Education*, 9(2), pp.145–163.
AID (Assessment for Instructional Development) is a behaviourally referenced class questionnaire developed from a data base drawn from 12 polytechnics and universities. It is intended to help the user to identify: (1) teaching objectives towards which the students lack confidence in their progress; (2) teaching behaviours that seem to bear on these objectives; and (3) changes of teaching strategy that may therefore help the students. AID is focused on individual classes and subjects. It is not suitable for 'accountability' uses. The paper describes the rationale for choosing a behaviourally referenced system rather than a 'satisfaction' scale, and the way AID was developed from earlier, mainly North American, behaviourally referenced systems. The characteristics and capabilities of the system are outlined and its use explained. Illustrations of three typical uses of the system are outlined: a comparison of the elements in a part-time course for use by the course team in a course review, and two analyses of particular teaching programmes for individual lecturers.

Donald, J.G. (1984) Quality indices for faculty evaluation. *Assessment and Evaluation in Higher Education*, 9(1), pp.41–52.
This paper surveys procedures and criteria for the evaluation of faculty in higher education. It first discusses the different indices currently in use for evaluating research, teaching and service activities. It then considers the use of these criteria in view of the shifting framework of evaluation in the

university from that based on promotion and tenure decisions to one which is based on institutional review. Finally, conditions for the success of faculty evaluation are outlined. These include evaluation procedures that are consultative in nature, the specification of criteria and standards, and an emphasis on the critical role of faculty in evaluation, and becoming evaluators themselves.

Donald, J.G. (1985) The state of research on university teaching effectiveness. *New directions for teaching and learning*, 23, pp.7–20.

Doyle, W. (1977) Paradigms for research on teacher effectiveness. *In* L.S. Shulman (ed) *Review of research in education.* Itasca, Ill.: Peacock.

Dunkin, M.J. and Barnes, J. (1986) Research on teaching in higher education. *In* M.C. Wittrock (ed) *Handbook of research on teaching*. New York: Macmillan, pp.754–77.

Eizenberg, N. (1986) Applying student learning research in practice. *In* J.A. Bowden (ed) *Student learning: research into practice*. Melbourne: University of Melbourne, pp.21–60.

Elliott, J. (1987) The great appraisal debate: some perspectives for research. *In Restructuring higher education: proceedings of the annual conference 1987, (ed.)* H. Eggins, Open University Press and SRHE, 1988, pp.151–182 Increasing state intervention in the control and distribution of the resources had placed teacher appraisal high on the agenda of the debate. Author considers that purpose to which the results of research into this issue are put. One of the major uses of such research is quoted as facilitating a negotiated consensus between apparently inconsistent points of view.

Elton, L. (1982) Assessment for Learning. *In* Bligh, D. (ed) *Professionalism and Flexibility in Learning*. Society for Research into Higher Education, Guildford pp.106–135.

Elton, L. (1984) Evaluating teaching and assessing teachers in universities. *Assessment and evaluation in higher education*, 9/2, Summer, pp.97–115.

Elton, L. (1987a) *Teaching in higher education: appraisal and training*. London: Kogan Page.

Elton, L. (1987b) UGC resource allocation and the assessment of teaching quality. Reprinted in L. Elton *Teaching in higher education: appraisal and training*. London: Kogan Page.

Elton, L. (1988) Appraisal and accountability in higher education. *Higher Education Quarterly*, Vol. 42, No. 3, Summer, pp.207–29.
Issue of external accountability linked to institutional appraisal rather than to appraisal of individual staff. Universities in past year concentrated on appraisal of individuals as Secretary of State indicated that without this he would not meet the current salary settlement. Staff allowed to formulate

own objectives for future on the basis of a self-appraisal of the past followed by a discussion and negotiation with appraisal. Importance shifting from research, to equal shares for excellence in teaching and administration. Competence, not to speak of excellence, in teaching and training should be judged on outlines based primarily on matters pertaining to curriculum design rather than on the sum total of individual classroom performances. Importance of teaching quality in any one institution does not lie primarily in the improvement of its individual teachers but in the improvement of its teaching as a whole, ie in good course design in widest sense and in teacher training – willingness of institutions to put resources into staff development and academic staff training to improve teaching function may be one of most important indicators of teaching quality in teaching. Problem with academic accountability lies in timescale and degree of precision of academics objectives. Some are short-term and fairly precise, others, speculative research programmes or body of graduates consonant with mission statement.

Entwistle, N. J., Hanley, M. and Hounsell, D. J. (1979) Identifying distinctive approaches to studying. *Higher Education* 8 pp.365–380.

Entwistle N. J. (1981) *Styles of Learning and Teaching: an integrated outline of educational psychology for students and lecturers.*

Entwistle, N. J. (1982) Study skills and independent learning. *Studies in Higher Education* Vol.7, No.1, pp.65–73.

Erdle, S. *et al* (1985) Personality, classroom behaviour and student ratings of college teaching effectiveness: a path analysis. *Journal of educational psychology*, 77, pp.394–407.

Feldens, M.G.F. and Duncan, J.K. (1986) Improving university teaching: what Brazilian students say about their teachers. *Higher Education* 15/6, pp.641–649.
A 72-item questionnaire gathered students' opinions about effective university teaching. 392 randomly selected, students of nursing, dentistry and medicine in Brazil were asked to bear in mind a particular teacher judged effective and to indicate on a Likert 5 point scale the degree to which that teacher exhibited the behaviour and/or attributes proposed by each of the 72 items. The students' responses were analysed to identify their teacher behaviour and for attributes most frequently and highly rated. A subsequent factor analysis identified 6 factors: student participation, classroom organization and management; teacher clarity; acceptance of students; punctuality and systemization. In terms of staff development these factors can be clustered into: improving interpersonal relationships; improving organization; management and evaluation; and enhancing knowledge and understanding.

Feldman, K.A. (1984) Class size and college students' evaluations of teachers and courses: a closer look. *Research in Higher Education*, 21 (1), pp.45–116.

The results of 52 studies that related class size to students' overall evaluations of teachers and to specific instructional or skill dimensions were compiled. Correlational analysis revealed only a slight inverse relationship between class size and overall (global) evaluations of teachers. The analysis likewise revealed only slight inverse relationships between class size and the communication/presentation dimensions of instruction (eg enthusiasm, knowledge of subject matter, clarity and understandableness, and organization and preparation). Larger inverse relationships were found between class size and interpersonal interaction dimensions of instruction (eg encouragement of open discussion, concern and respect for students, availability, and helpfulness). The rating dimensions of the first type were highly intercorrelated and had stronger positive associations with the overall evaluations than did the rating dimensions of the second type.

Field, M. (1987) Preparing for staff appraisal. *Coombe Lodge Report*, 19/10.

Fox, D. (1983) Personal theories of teaching. *Studies in higher education*, 8, pp.511–535.

Fox, D. (1984) What counts as teaching. *Assessment and evaluation in higher education*, 9/2, Summer, pp.133–43.

Furumark, A.M. (1980) Institutional self-evaluation in Sweden. Reprinted in M. Kogan (ed) *Evaluating higher education*. London: Jessica Kingsley, pp.74–83.

Gibbs, G. (1983) *Guide to submitting teaching profiles for promotion*. Oxford: Oxford Polytechnic Educational Methods Unit.

Gibbs, G. (1988) *Learning by Doing*. London: Further Education Unit.

Gibson, A. (1986) Inspecting education. *In* G. Moodie (ed) *Standards and criteria in higher education*. Guildford: SRHE and NFER/Nelson.

Glover, D. (1990) *Enterprise in Higher Education: a briefing for employers*. Cambridge: CRAC.

Goodlad, S. (1988) Four Forms of Heresy in Higher Education: aspects of academic freedom in education for the professions. *In* Tight, M. (ed) *Academic Freedom and Responsibility*. Milton Keynes: SRHE/Open University Press, pp.49–65.

Gross, R.B. and Small, A.C. (1979) A survey of faculty opinions about student evaluation of instructors. *Teaching of psychology*, 6, pp.216–19.

Hale, Sir E. (Chairman) (1964) *Report of the Committee on university teaching methods*. London: HMSO.

Hewton, E. (1982) *Rethinking Educational Change: A case for diplomacy*. Guildford: Society for Research into Higher Education.

Hort, L. K. (1988) Staff Assessment: The Development of Procedures for Australian Universities. *Assessment and Evaluation in Higher Education* Vol. 13, No. 1, pp.73–78.

Hildebrand, M.R.C. *et al* (1971) *Evaluating university teaching*. Berkeley, Ca: Berkeley Centre for Research and Development in Higher Education.

HMI (1990) *A Survey of Validation and Review. Arrangements of CNAA Courses*. DES (Ref 58/90/NS).

HMSO (1987) Cmnd 114 *Higher education: meeting the challenge*. London: HMSO.

HMSO (1985) Cmnd 9524 *Development of higher education into the 1990s* [The Green Paper]. London: HMSO.

Hodgson, V. (1984) Learning from lectures. *In* F. Marton *et al* (eds) *The experience of learning*. Edinburgh: Scottish Academic Press.

Hudson, H.R. (Chairman) (1986) *Review of efficiency and effectiveness in higher education*. Canberra: Australian Government Publishing Service.

Jarratt, A. (Chairman) (1985) *Report of the Steering Committee for Efficiency Studies in Universities*. London: CVCP.

Jones, A. (1988) The Manpower Services Commission's Enterprise in Higher Education initiative. *Industry and Higher Education*. 2 (2), pp.117–119.

Jones, J. *et al* (1985) Students' expectations of good teachers: primary, secondary and tertiary views. Paper presented at NZARE Conference, Auckland, New Zealand.

Jones, J. (1989) Students' ratings of teacher personality and teaching competence. *Higher education*, 18, pp.551–8.

Knapper, C.K. (1984) Changing course in midstream. *Instructional development at Waterloo*, 18.

Knowles, M. (1975) *Self-directed Learning: a guide for learners and teachers*. Association Press.

Knowles, M. *et al* (1986) *Using Learning Contracts*. San Francisco: Jossey-Bass.

Kogan, M. (1988) Learning to square up to PIs. *THES*, no. 806, 15 April, p.15.

Kogan, M. (ed) (1989) *Evaluating higher education*. London: Jessica Kingsley.

Kolb, D. (1984) *Experiential Learning: experience as the source of learning and development*. Englewood Cliffs, N.J: Prentice-Hall.

Lane, J.E. and Frederiksson, B. (1983) *Higher education and public administration*. Stockholm: Almqvist and Wiksell.

Laurillard, D. M. (1979) The process of student learning. *Higher Education* 8. pp.395–409.

Leverhulme Report (1983) *Excellence in diversity: towards a new strategy for higher education*. Guildford: SRHE.

Lindop, Sir N. (Chairman) (1985) *Academic validation in public sector higher education: the report of the Committee of Enquiry into the academic validation of degree courses in public sector higher education*. (Cmnd 9501) London: HMSO.

Loder C. P. J. (1984) 'An Exploratory Study of Final Year Undergraduate Students' Examination Preparation Techniques' (unpublished MA dissertation, Lancaster University.)

Lowman, J. (1984) *Mastering the techniques of teaching*. San Francisco: Jossey-Bass.

Lublin, J. and Barrand, J. (1987) What the lecturer can teach us. *Research and development in higher education*, 9, pp.5–11.

Macnair, G. (1990) The British Enterprise in Higher Education Initiative. *Higher Education Management* 2 (1), pp.60-71.

Marsh, D.C.(1982) The production model of quality control and its application to human resources in education. *Coombe Lodge Report* Vol.15, No.5, pp.184–192.

Marsh, H.W. (1980) The influence of student, course and instructor characteristics on evaluation of university teaching. *American educational research journal*, 17, pp.219–37.

Marsh, H.W. (1984) Students evaluation of university teaching: dimensionality, reliability, validity, potential biases and utility. *Journal of educational psychology*, 76, pp.707–54.

Mathias, H. (1984) The evaluation of university teaching: context values and innovation. *Assessment and evaluation in higher education*, 9/2, Summer, pp.79–96.

Marton, F., Hounsell, D., and Entwistle, N., (eds) *The Experience of Learning*. Edinburgh: Scottish Academic Press.

McBean, A. and Al-Nassri, S. (1982) Questionnaire design for student measurement of teaching effectiveness. *Higher Education*, 11(3), pp.273–288.
   The literature on the design of questionnaires to be used for student evaluation of teaching effectiveness is reviewed. Problems of construction and interpretation of such questionnaires are described. A questionnaire developed by the authors for use at the Faculty of Engineering at the University of Waterloo is given as an example which overcomes many of the difficulties.

McBean, E.A. and Lennox, C. (1982) Issues of teaching effectiveness as observed via course critiques. *Higher Education*, 11(6), pp.645–655.

For more than ten years, course and teaching evaluation questionnaires have been completed by students within engineering at the University of Waterloo. The distribution and collection of questionnaires is conducted by the Undergraduate Engineering Society of the university. The responses of students to the questionnaires are examined in this article with respect to their willingness to complete the questionnaires, the variability of teacher ratings over time, and the utility to the university administration of the obtained responses. It is claimed that the greatest value of the questionnaires is, perhaps, in the 'flagging' of courses and/or teachers that are in difficulty.

McClain, C., Krueger, D., and Taylor, T. (1986) Northeast Missouri State University Value-Added Assessment Program: a model of educational accountability. *International Journal of Institutional Management in Higher Education* Vol. 10 No. 3, pp.252–271.

McConnell, D. and Hodgson, V. (1985) The development of student constructed lecture feedback questionnaires. *Assessment and evaluation in higher education*, 10, pp.2–28.

McCready D.J. (1981) Student evaluation of teaching. *Canadian Journal of Higher Education*, 11(2), pp.67–77.

The analysis of factors which influence student valuations of teaching is the subject of this paper. An empirical test, using the evaluations carried out in the School of Business and Economics at Wilfrid Laurier University shows that the grades granted by instructors do not relate significantly to the evaluations of that instructor by students. Factors which do relate to higher evaluations include: early morning classes, small classes, optional subjects, and senior classes. From a survey of how faculty react to the evaluations, it appears that most faculty do not find the evaluations useful in making improvements in their own teaching.

McKeachie, W.J. (1979) Student rating of faculty: a reprise. *AAUP bulletin*, pp.394–97.

McKeachie, W.J. *et al* (1980) Using student ratings and consultation to improve instruction. *British journal of education psychology*, 50, pp.168–74.

Miller, A.H. (1988) Student assessment of teaching in higher education. *Higher Education* Vol. 17, No.1, pp.3–15.

Miller, R. (1972) *Evaluating Faculty Performance*. San Francisco: Jossey-Bass.

Miller, R. (1974) *Developing Programs for Faculty Evaluation: a source book for higher education*. San Francisco: Jossey-Bass.

Miller, R. (1979) *The Assessment of College Performance: a handbook of techniques and measures for institutional self-evaluation*. San Francisco: Jossey-Bass.

Miller, R. (1987) *Evaluating Faculty for Promotion and Tenure*. San Francisco: Jossey-Bass.

Millman, J. (ed) (1981) *Handbook of teacher education*. Newbury Park, Ca: Sage.

Moodie, G.C. (1986) Fit for what? *In* G.C. Moodie (ed) *Standards and criteria in higher education*. Guildford: SRHE & NFER/Nelson.

Moodie, G. (1988) The Debates about Higher Education Quality in Britain and USA. *Studies in Higher Education* Vol. 13 No. 1.
In Britain 'quality' has been set alongside 'value for money' as a policy goal in higher education. The debate in the USA, by contrast, pairs 'quality' with 'equity', 'equality', or 'access'. For the most part, the public debate in Britain has lacked two other elements that are conspicuous in the American one; discussion of curricular content (eg the nature of liberal education and the plight of the 'humanities') and references to hard evidence about either the decline or maintenance of standards. There is, of course, much common ground – eg. the need for more good mathematicians and technologists. The principal reasons for the different forms the debate has taken are (broadly) political and structural. Nevertheless, the debate in each country can benefit from knowledge of the other's problems, practices, and principles.

Moses, I. (1985) Academic development units and the improvement of teaching. *Higher Education*, 14(1), pp.75–100.
A survey was conducted in 1983 of those educational development practices which directors of educational development units in Australia found most effective in their institutions. Responses were received from 17 out of 23 directors approached. A wide variety of responses were given which are discussed. The second part of the article is a report on a series of over 100 interviews with academic staff at the University of Queensland concerning their views on academic staff development. Quantitative data is not given, but it is averred that all staff, whether they had participated in workshops or not, were favourably disposed to professional development. Most staff wanted practical advice, prescriptive guidelines and structure in organized staff development sessions. Most staff saw greater evaluation as the best way of encouraging excellence in teaching. In the third section the staff development programme at the University of Queensland is discussed.

Moses, I. (1985b) High quality teaching in a university: identification and description. *Studies in higher education*, 10/3, pp.301–313.

Moses, I. (1986b) Student evaluation of teaching in an Australian university: staff perceptions and reactions. *Assessment and evaluation in higher education*, 11/2, pp.117–29.

Moses, I. (1987) Educational Development Units: a cross-cultural perspective. *Higher education*, 16/4, pp.449–79.

Moses, I. (1988) *Academic Evaluation and Development, A University Case Study*. St Lucia: University of Queensland Press.

Moses, I. (1989) Role and problems of heads of departments in performance appraisal. *Assessment and evaluation in higher education*, 14/2, Summer, pp.95–105.

MSC (Manpover Services Commission) (1987) *Enterprise in Higher Education: guidelines for applicants*. Sheffield: MSC.

Murray, H.G. (1980) *Evaluating university teaching: a review of research*. Toronto: Ontario Confederation of University Faculty Associations.

Murray, H.G. (1984) The impact of formative and summative evaluation of teaching in North American universities. *Assessment and evaluation in higher education*, 9/2, Summer, pp.117–32.

Murray, H.G. and Newby, W.G. (1982) Faculty attitudes toward evaluation of teaching at the University of Western Ontario. *Assessment and Evaluation in Higher Education*, 7/2, pp.144–151.
At the University of Western Ontario the evaluation of teaching as a basis for administrative decisions on staff salary, tenure and promotion has been mandatory for 12 years. A questionnaire survey of views about the evaluation of teaching was carried out among the 1268 full-time academics, of whom 53 per cent completed the questionnaire. Chi-square goodness-of-fit tests showed that the respondents were representative of the faculty as a whole in terms of academic rank, sex, faculty affiliation and length of service.

The only widespread method of evaluating classroom instruction was the use of student ratings. (The use of undergraduate students' ratings in their own department was reported by 93 per cent of the staff.) Staff, and students in a parallel survey, agreed on the five characteristics of effective teaching which were rated to highest importance: stimulation of student learning, clarity of classroom presentation, knowledge of subject matter, quality of course content, and fair and constructive assessment of student performance. Staff and students also agreed that students were the best judges of the first two characteristics and that staff were the best judges of the third and fourth. Opinion was divided as to whether students or staff colleagues were best qualified to judge the assessment of student performance.

Providing diagnostic feedback for the improvement of teaching was rated by 78 per cent of faculty respondents as a highly important goal for teaching evaluation; 71 per cent stated that student evaluation of classroom teaching provides useful feedback for self-improvement. The use of evaluation data in salary, promotion and tenure decisions was seen as a legitimate purpose of evaluation by 71 per cent of respondents who agreed that the practice should be compulsory; 60 per cent agreed that student evaluations were suitable for use in making these decisions.

The paper also reports the more detailed views of staff on the current system for the evaluation of teaching and the prospects for its development.

NAB 4 (National Advisory Body for Local Authority Higher Education) (1984) *Quality*. London: NAB (mimeo).

Neave, G. (1986) The all-seeing eye of the prince in Western Europe. *In* G.C. Moodie (ed) *Standards and criteria in higher education*. Guildford: SRHE & NFER/Nelson, pp.157–70.

Nisbet, J. (1986a) Staff and standards. *In* G.C. Moodie (ed) *Standards and criteria in higher education*. Guildford: SRHE & NFER/Nelson, pp.90–106.

Nisbet, J. (1986b) Appraisal for improvement. *In* E. Stones and B. Wilcox (eds) *Appraising appraisal*. Birmingham: British Educational Research Association, pp.10–19.

Nuttall, D. (1986) What can we learn from research on teaching and appraisal? *In* E. Stones and B. Wilcox *Appraising appraisal*. Birmingham: British Educational Research Association, pp.20–28.

Outcalt, D.L. (ed) (1980) *Report of the task force on teaching evaluation* Berkeley: University of California.

Overall, J.U. and Marsh, H.W. (1979) Mid-term feedback from students: its relationship to instructional improvement and students' cognitive and affective outcomes. *Journal of educational psychology*, 71, pp.856–65.

Pearson, R., Pike, G., Gordon, A. and Weyman, C. (1989) *How many graduates in the 21st century?, the Choice is Yours:* IMS Report No 177. Brighton, Sussex: Council for Industry and Higher Education/Institute of Manpower Studies.

Percy, K. and Ramsden, P. (1980) *Independent Study: Two examples from English Higher Education*. Guildford: Society for Research into Higher Education.

Perry, P. (1987) Accountability and Inspection in Higher Education. *Higher Education Quarterly* Vol. 41 No. 4, pp.344–353.

Pollitt, C. (1987) The politics of performance assessment: lessons for higher education. *Studies in Higher Education* Vol. 12 No. 1.

Price, C. (1989) Academics and Society: freedom's seamless robe. *In* Ball, C. and Eggins, H. (eds) *Higher Education into the 1990s: New Dimensions*. Milton Keynes: SRHE/Open University Press, pp.51–62.

Ramsden, P. (1979) Student learning and perceptions of the academic environment. *Higher Education* 8 pp.411–427.

Ramsden, P. (1985) Student Experience of Learning. *In* Jacques, D. and Richardson, J. (eds) *The Future for Higher Education*. Guildford: SRHE and NFER Nelson.

Ramsden, P. and Entwistle, N. (1981) Effects of academic departments on students' approaches to studying. *British Journal of Educational Psychology* 51.

Renner, R.R. *et al* (1986) Responsible behaviour as effective teaching: a new look at student rating of professors. *Assessment and evaluation in higher education*, 11/2, pp.138–45.
Items in student rating instruments unavoidably contain bias in favour of particular concepts of excellence which make them invalid for measuring the teaching effectiveness of a wide variety of college instructors. The use of scores from such instruments to penalize or reward faculty in salary, tenure and promotion decisions may adversely affect dedicated instruction. Given this problem, an alternative is proposed in which students report whether instructors acted responsibly rather than excellently. Proposed is a two-part instrument which uses students to monitor acceptable employee behaviours in teaching settings to satisfy management needs, while at the same time providing qualitative feedback to the instructor for the purpose of self-improvement.

Riegel, R.P. and Rhodes, D.M. (1985) Anonymity in the academy: the case of faculty evaluation. *Educational theory*, 135/3, Summer, pp.304–5.

Robbins, D. (1988) *The Rise of Independent Study*. Milton Keynes: SRHE/Open University Press.

Roe, E., McDonald, R. and Moses, I. (1986) *Reviewing Academic Performance*. St. Lucia: University of Queensland Press.

Rogers, C.R. (1983) *Freedom to Learn: a view of what education might become*. Columbus, Ohio: Charles E. Merrill.

Royal Society of Arts (1990) *More Means Different*. London: RSA.

Rushton, J.P. and Murray, H.G. (1985) On the assessment of teaching effectiveness in British universities. *Bulletin of the British Psychological Society*, 38, pp.361–5.
This paper selectively reviews a sampling of the vast literature on teaching effectiveness in North American universities. More thorough coverage is provided by McKeachie (1979) and Murray (1980). However, it should be apparent that a variety of research projects can be undertaken in this important area without inordinate difficulty or effort. The paper concludes that it would be of great interest to see if teaching evaluation results discovered in the North American context are generalizable to their rather different situation in Britain.

Rutherford, D. (1982) Developing university teaching: a strategy for revitaliz-
ation. *Higher Education*, 11(2), pp.177–191.
  Institutional policies and practices aimed at developing university teaching
  are analysed according to various theoretical perspectives which seek to
  explain why some innovations are successful and others are not. Within this
  framework the role of academic staff employed on a full- or part-time basis
  to support such development is also examined. Following from this analysis
  a coherent strategy to facilitate the improvement of university teaching is
  proposed.

Rutherford, D. (1987a) Indicators of performance: reactions and issues.
Assessment and evaluation in higher education, 12/2, summer, pp.94–104.
  In response to the Jarratt Report, this paper analyses the results from a
  series of structured interviews with academic staff at the University of
  Birmingham to proposals for appraising individual and departmental
  performance in teaching, research and administration; and highlights
  current attitudes, concerns and practices which tend to inhibit discussion of
  the career development of individual academics and institutional planning.
  Three key issues are also explored: the purpose of the appraisal; precisely
  what should be appraised; and who should be responsible. It is concluded
  that the most likely development is the implementation of a system of
  Indicators of Performance to monitor 'institutional health' and serve as a
  guide to long-term planning.

Rutherford, D. (1987b) Indicators of performance: some practical suggestions. *Assessment and evaluation in higher education*, 12/1, Spring, pp.46–
55.
  Universities are coming under increasing pressure to develop and implement indicators of performance in order to demonstrate their efficiency and
  to facilitate institutional planning. In this paper a number of possible
  indicators for monitoring individual and departmental performance in
  teaching and research are explored. Preliminary studies indicate that while
  it is possible to identify both 'excellence' and relatively poor performance, it
  is very difficult, at least in the present circumstances, to effect positive
  changes in the latter. A sensitive yet economical system of indicators of
  performance could ensure that the professional development of individual
  academics, as well as departmental and institutional planning, could
  proceed on a more realistic and rational basis.

Rutherford, D. (1987c) Performance appraisal: strategies for implementation
in universities. *Educational change and development*, 8/1, pp.15–18.
  In the wake of the Jarratt Report there is widespread acceptance among
  academics at the University of Birmingham that more systematic procedures for performance appraisal are necessary. It is probable that self-
  appraisal will be the natural starting point for the appraisal of individual
  performance followed by an annual interview with the head of department

or other senior colleague. This paper explores strategies for the implementation of performance appraisal.

Rutherford, D (1988) Performance appraisal: a survey of academic staff opinion. *Studies in higher education*, 13/1, pp.89–100.
This paper reports the results from a questionnaire which sought the opinions of a representative sample of academic staff at the University of Birmingham to the introduction of more regular and systematic performance appraisal in universities. In particular, whether respondents were of the opinion that further procedures for the appraisal of individuals and departments were necessary and, if so, who should be involved in such appraisals. In addition, the reactions of staff to the suggestions for an Individual Annual Review – providing a focus for career development – and a Departmental Annual Report – bringing together a detailed analysis of a department's past performance with an academic plan for its immediate future – are explored. Finally, some opinions on the role of heads of departments and external examiners, and some information on the range of methods of performance appraisal currently in use are presented. The data is further analysed on the basis of the respondents' faculty, position and years of service in universities. Respondents were invited to complete the questionnaire on the understanding that the main focus of appraisal was the professional development of individuals and departments, and that the purpose of the survey was to inform and influence policy-making in the university.

Ryan, J.J. *et al* (1980) Student evaluation: the faculty responds. *Research in higher education*, 12, pp.317–333.

Scriven, M. (1981) Summative teacher evaluation. *In* J. Millman (ed) *Handbook of teacher evaluation*. Beverly Hills: Sage.

Seldin, P. (1980) *Successful faculty evaluation programs*. New York: Coventry.

Seldin, P. (1982) Improving Faculty Evaluation Systems. *Peabody Journal of Education* Vol. 59 No. 2, pp.93–99.

Seldin, P. (1984) *Changing practices in faculty evaluation: a critical assessment and recommendations for improvement*. San Francisco: Jossey-Bass.

Seldin, P. (1986) *Evaluating teaching performance*. Workshop presented at the University of Maryland, College Park, February

Seldin, P. (1988) Evaluating college teaching. *New directions for teaching and learning*, 33, pp.47–56.

Silver, H. (1980) *Education and the Social Condition*. Methuen: London.

Silver, H. (1987) From Great Expectations to Bleak House. *Higher Education Quarterly* Vol. 41 No. 3, pp.205–224.

Silver, H. and Brennan, J. (1988) *A Liberal Vocationalism.* London: Methuen.

Silver, H. and Silver, P. (1986) The escaping answer. *In* G.C. Moodie (ed) *Standards and criteria in higher education.* Guildford: SRHE & NFER/ Nelson.

Sissom, L.E. (1982) Faculty evaluation and reward: does effective teaching matter? *Engineering Education*, 72, pp.380–384.
Evaluation of faculty members serves two functions: recognition and reward: and personal growth and improvement. Although teaching, research and publication, and personal qualifications are the most frequently cited evaluation criteria, data suggest that research is increasingly rewarded to the detriment of teaching effectiveness. In general, good teaching is likely to be the least rewarded area because everyone is assumed to be able to teach, teaching ability is difficult to measure, and a teaching reputation is usually recognized only locally. Research skills are more widely recognized because research output is more visible and easily quantified. Public service performance is usually locally recognised and difficult to assess. A 1972–73 national study of faculty members revealed that, in the fields of mathematics and civil and electrical engineering, publications were rewarded across all fields, public service rewards were nonuniform and outstanding teaching was not rewarded.

Sizer, J. (1982) Performance indicators for institutions of higher education under conditions of financial stringency, contraction and changing needs. *In* R. McCormick (ed) *Calling education to account.* London: Heinemann, pp.66–77.

Squires, G. (1990) *First Degree: the undergraduate curriculum.* Milton Keynes: SRHE and Open University Press.

Smith, P. *et al* (1988) *Alternatives for developing teaching effectiveness.* Seattle: Pacific University School of Education.

Staropoli, A. (1986) Le Comité National d'Evaluation: an innovation in French higher education. Reprinted *in* M. Kogan *Evaluating higher education.* London: Jessica Kingsley, pp.116–21.

Sutherland, M.B. (1980) Can university teaching be evaluated. *Teaching News* (Queen's University, Belfast, November)

Swinnerton-Dyer, P. (1985) UGC circular letter 22/85, 19 November. London: UGC.

Tague, B. (Chairman) (1982) *Tenure of academics: report of the Senate Standing Committee on Education and the Arts.* Canberra: Australian Government Publishing Services.

Taylor, W. (1987) *Universities Under Scrutiny.* Paris: OECD.

Trow, M. (1987) Academic Standards and Mass Higher Education. *Higher Education Quarterly* Vol. 41 No. 3.

UGC (1984) *A strategy for higher education into the 1990s*. London: HMSO.

Wagner, L. (1989) Access and Standards: an unresolved (and unresolvable?) debate. *In* Ball, C. and Eggins, H (eds) *Higher Education into the 1990s: new directions*. Milton Keynes: SRHE/Open University Press pp.29–37.

Warren Piper, D. (1985) Enquiry into the role of external examiners. *Studies in Higher Education* Vol. 10. No. 3, pp.331–342.

Webster, D.S. (1985) Does Research Productivity Enhance Teaching? *Educational Record* Vol. 66, pp.60–62.

Weiner, M. (1981) *English Culture and the Decline of the Industrial Spirit, 1850–1980*. Cambridge: Cambridge University Press.

Weil, S. and McGill, I. (eds) (1989) Making Sense of Experiential Learning: diversity in theory and practice. Milton Keynes: SRHE/Open University Press.

Wheeler, G. C. (1982) The implications of process of quality control in further and higher education. *Coombe Lodge Report* Vol.15, No.5, pp.179–183.

Williams, B.R. (1979) *Education, training and employment: report of the Committee of Inquiry into Education and Training*. Canberra: Australian Government Publishing Service.

Williams, G. (1986) The missing bottom line. *In* G.C. Moodie (ed) *Standards and criteria in higher education*. Guildford: SRHE & NFER/Nelson.

Williams, G. and Blackstone, T. (1983) *Response to adversity: higher education in a harsh climate*. Guildford: SRHE.

Wilson, T.C. (1988) Student evaluation-of-teaching forms: a critical perspective. *Review of higher education*, 12/1, Autumn, pp.79–95.

Wise, A., Darling Hammond, L., McLaughlin, M. and Bernstein, H. (1984) *Teacher Evaluation: a study of effective practices*. Santa Monica, California: Rand Corporation.

Wright, P. W. G. (1988): Rethinking the Arms of Higher Education. *In* H. Eggins (ed) *Restructuring Higher Education: the Proceedings of the Annual conference of the Society for Research into Higher Education, 1987*. Milton Keynes: Open University Press.

Wright, P.W.G. (1989) Access or exclusion? some comments on the history and future prospects of continuing education in England. *Studies in Higher Education* Vol. 14 No. 1, pp.23–40.

Note: Abstracts have been provided for those books and articles that are considered to be of particular interest and use and where access may be difficult.

Index